The King of Pirates by Daniel Defoe

Being an Account of the Famous Enterprises of Captain Avery, the Mock King of Madagascar

WITH

His RAMBLES and PIRACIES; wherein all the Sham ACCOUNTS formerly publish'd of him, are detected.

In Two LETTERS from himself; one during his Stay at Madagascar, and one since his Escape from thence.

Daniel Defoe is most well-known for his classic novels *Robinson Crusoe* and *Moll Flanders*. Born around 1660, he was also a journalist, a pamphleteer, a businessman, a spy. His life was long and colourful, and the breadth of his work, still highly regarded, is infused with similar vigour.

It is said that only the bible has been printed in more languages than Robinson Crusoe. Defoe is also noted for being one of the earliest proponents of the novel. He was extremely prolific and a very versatile writer, producing several hundred books, pamphlets, and journals on various topics including politics, crime, religion, marriage, psychology and the supernatural. He was also a pioneer of economic journalism though was made bankrupt on more on one occasion and usually mired in debt.

In later life Defoe was often most seen on Sundays when bailiffs and the like could legally make no move on him. Allegedly it was whilst hiding from creditors that he died on April 24th, 1731. He was interred in Bunhill Fields, London.

Index of contents

THE PREFACE

One of the particular Advantages of the following Letters from Captain Avery, is, the Satisfaction they will give the Readers how much they have been impos'd upon in the former ridiculous and extravagant Accounts which have been put upon the World in what has been publish'd already.

It has been enough to the Writers of this Man's Life, as they call it, that they could put any Thing together, to make a kind of monstrous unheard of Story, as romantick as the Reports that have been spread about of him; and the more those Stories appear'd monstrous and incredible, the more suitable they seem'd to be to what the World would have been made to expect of Captain Avery.

There is always a great Deference between what Men say of themselves, and what others say for them, when they come to write Historically of the Transactions of their Lives.

The Publisher of these Letters recommends this Performance to the Readers, to make their Judgment of the Difference between them and the extravagant Stories already told, and which is most likely to be genuine; and, as they verily believe these Letters to be the best and truest Account of Captain Avery's Piracies, that ever has or ever will come to the Knowledge of the World, they recommend them as such, and doubt not but they will answer for themselves in the Reading.

The Account given of Captain Avery's taking the Great Mogul's Daughter, ravishing and murdering her, and all the Ladies of her Retinue, is so differently related here, and so extravagantly related before, that it cannot but be a Satisfaction to the most unconcern'd Reader, to find such a horrible Piece of Villainy as the other was suppos'd to be, not to have been committed in the World.

On the contrary, we find here, that except plundering that Princess of her Jewels and Money to a prodigious Value, a Thing which, falling into the Hands of Freebooters, every one that had the Misfortune to fall into such Hands would expect: But, that excepting this, the Lady was used with all the Decency and Humanity, and, perhaps, with more than ever Women, falling among Pirates, had found before; especially considering that, by Report, she was a most beautiful and agreeable Person herself, as were also several of those about her.

The Booty taken with her, tho' infinitely great in itself, yet has been so magnify'd beyond common Sense, that it makes all the rest that has been said of those Things ridiculous and absurd.

The like Absurdity in the former Relations of this Matter, is that of the making an Offer of I know not how many Millions to the late Queen, for Captain Avery's Pardon, with a Petition to the Queen, and her Majesty's negative Answer; all which are as much true as his being Master of so many Millions if Money, which he nor his Gang never had; and of his being proclaim'd King of Madagascar; marrying the Mogul's Daughter, and the like: And, by the Bye, it was but ill laid together of those who publish'd, that he first ravish'd her, then murder'd her, and then marry'd her; all which are very remarkable for the recommending the Thing to those that read it.

If these Stories are explain'd here, and duly expos'd, and the History of Captain Avery set in a fairer Light, the End is answer'd; and of this the Readers are to be the only Judges: But this may be said, without any Arrogance, that this Story, stripp'd of all the romantick, improbable, and impossible Parts of it, looks more like the History of Captain Avery, than any Thing yet publish'd ever has done; and, if it is not prov'd that the Captain wrote these Letters himself, the Publisher says, None but the Captain himself will ever be able to mend them.

THE KING OF PIRATES

THE FIRST LETTER

You may be sure I receiv'd with Resentment enough the Account, that a most ridiculous Book, entitled, My Life and Adventures, had been publish'd in England, being fully assur'd nothing of Truth could be contain'd in such a Work; and tho' it may be true, that my extravagant Story may be the proper Foundation of a Romance, yet as no Man has a Title to publish it better than I have to expose and contradict it, I send you this by one of my particular Friends, who having an Opportunity of returning into England, has promis'd to convey it faithfully to you; by which, at least, two Things shall be made good to the World; first, that they shall be satisfy'd in the scandalous and unjust Manner in which others have already treated me, and it shall give, in the mean Time, a larger Account of what may at present be fit to be made publick, of my unhappy tho' successful Adventures.

I shall not trouble my Friends with any Thing of my Original and first Introduction into the World, I leave it to you to add from yourself what you think proper to be known on that Subject; only this I enjoin you to take Notice of, that the Account printed of me, with all the Particulars of my Marriage, my being defrauded, and leaving my Family and native Country on that Account, is a meer Fable and a made Story, to embellish, as the Writer of it perhaps suppos'd, the rest of his Story, or perhaps to fill up the Book, that it might swell to a Magnitude which his barren Invention could not supply.

In the present Account, I have taken no Notice of my Birth, Infancy, Youth, or any of that Part; which, as it was the most useless Part of my Years to myself so 'tis the most useless to any one that shall read this Work to know, being altogether barren of any Thing remarkable in it self, or instructing to others: It is sufficient to me to let the World know, as above, that the former Accounts, made publick, are utterly false, and to begin my Account of myself at a Period which may be more useful and entertaining.

It may be true, that I may represent some Particulars of my Life, in this Tract, with Reserve, or Enlargement, such as may be sufficient to conceal any Thing in my present Circumstance that ought to be conceal'd and reserv'd, with Respect to my own Safety; and therefore, if on Pretence of Justice the busy World should look for me in one Part of the World when I am in another, search for my new Kingdom in Madagascar, and should not find it, or search for my Settlement on one Side of the Island, when it lies on another, they must not take this ill; for Self-preservation being the supreme Law of Nature, all Things of this Kind must submit to that.

In Order then to come immediately to my Story, I shall, without any Circumlocutions, give you Leave to tell the World, that being bred to the Sea from a Youth, none of those romantick Introductions publish'd had any Share in my Adventures, or were any way the Cause of my taking the Courses I have since been embark'd in: But as in several Parts of my wandring Life I had seen something of the immense Wealth, which the Buccaneers, and other Adventurers, met with in their scouring about the World for Purchase, I had, for a long Time, meditated in my Thoughts to get possess'd of a good Ship for that Purpose, if I could, and to try my Fortune. I had been some Years in the Bay of Campeachy, and tho' with Patience I endur'd the Fatigue of that laborious Life, yet it was as visible to others as to myself, that I was not form'd by Nature for a Logwood-Cutter, any more than I was for a Foremast-man; and therefore Night and Day I apply'd myself to study how I should dismiss myself from that Drudgery, and get to be, first or last, Master of a good Ship, which was the utmost of my Ambition at that Time; resolving, in the mean Time, that when ever any such Thing should happen, I would try my Fortune in the Cruising Trade, but would be sure not to prey upon my own Countrymen.

It was many Years after this before I could bring my Purposes to pass; and I serv'd, first, in some of the Adventures of Captain Sharp, Captain Sawkins, and others, in their bold Adventures in the South Seas, where I got a very good Booty; was at the taking of Puna, where we were oblig'd to leave infinite Wealth behind us, for want of being able to bring it away; and after several Adventures in those Seas, was among that Party who fought their Way Sword in Hand thro' all the Detachments of the Spaniards, in the Journey over Land, cross the Isthmus of Darien, to the North Seas; and when other of our Men gat away, some one Way, some another, I, with twelve more of our Men, by Help of a Periagua, gat into the Bay of Campeachy, where we fell very honestly to cutting of Logwood, not for Want, but to employ ourselves till we could make off.

Here three of our Men dy'd, and we that were left, shar'd their Money among us; and having stay'd here two Years, without seeing any Way of Escape that I dar'd to trust to, I at last, with two of our Men, who spoke Spanish perfectly well, made a desperate Attempt to travel over Land to L— having bury'd all our Money, (which was worth eight thousand Pieces of Eight a Man, tho' most of it in Gold) in a Pit in the Earth which we dug twelve Foot deep, and where it would have lyen still, for no Man knew where to look for it; but we had an Opportunity to come at it again some Years after.

We travell'd along the Sea-shore five Days together, the Weather exceeding hot, and did not doubt but we should so disguise ourselves as to be taken for Spaniards; but our better Fortune provided otherwise for us, for the sixth Day of our March we found a Canoe lying on the Shore with no one in her: We found, however, several Things in her, which told us plainly that she belong'd to some Englishmen who were on Shore; so we resolv'd to sit down by her and wait: By and by we heard the Englishmen, who were seven in Number, and were coming back to their Boat, having been up the Country to an Ingenio, where they had gotten great Quantities of Provision, and were bringing it down to their Boat which they had left on the Shore, (with the Help of five Indians, of whom they had bought it) not thinking there was any People thereabouts: When they saw us, not knowing who we were, they were just going to fire at us; when I, perceiving it, held up a white Flag as high as I could reach it, which was, in short, only a Piece of an old Linnen Wastcoat which I had on, and pull'd it off for the Occasion; upon this, however, they forbore firing at us, and when they came nearer to us, they could easily see that we were their own Countrymen: They enquir'd of us what we came there for; we told them, we had travell'd from Campeachy, where being tir'd with the Hardships of our Fortune, and not getting any Vessel to carry us where we durst go, we were even desperate, and cared not what became of us; so that had not they came to us thus happily, we should have put our selves into the Hands of the Spaniards rather than have perish'd where we were.

They took us into their Boat, and afterwards carry'd us on Board their Ship; when we came there, we found they were a worse Sort of Wanderers than ourselves, for tho' we had been a Kind of Pyrates, known and declar'd Enemies to the Spaniards, yet it was to them only, and to no other; for we never offer'd to rob any of our other European Nations, either Dutch or French, much less English; but now we were listed in the Service of the Devil indeed, and, like him, were at War with all Mankind.

However, we not only were oblig'd to sort with them, while with them, but in a little Time the Novelty of the Crime wore off, and we grew harden'd to it, like the rest: And in this Service I spent four Years more of my Time.

Our Captain in this Pirate Ship was nam'd Nichols, but we call'd him Captain Redhand; it seems it was a Scots Sailor gave him that Name, when he was not the Head of the Crew, because he was so bloody a Wretch, that he scarce ever was at the taking any Prize, but he had a Hand in some Butchery or other.

They were hard put to it for fresh Provisions, or they would not have sent thus up into the Country a single Canoe; and when I came on Board they were so straiten'd, that, by my Advice, they resolv'd to go to the Isle of Cuba to kill wild Beef, of which the South Side of the Island is so full: Accordingly we sail'd thither directly.

The Vessel carry'd sixteen Guns, but was fitted to carry twenty two, and there was on Board one hundred and sixty stout Fellows, as bold and as case-harden'd for the Work as ever I met with upon any Occasion whatever: We victual'd in this Place for eight Months, by our Calculation; but our Cook, who had the Management of the Salting and Pickling the Beef, order'd his Matters so, that had he been let alone he would have starv'd us all, and poison'd us too; for as we are oblig'd to hunt the black Cattle in the Island sometimes a great while before we can shoot them, it should be observ'd, that the Flesh of those that are heated before they are kill'd, is not fit to be pickled or salted up for Keeping.

But this Man happening to pickle up the Beef, without Regard to this particular Distinction, most of the Beef, so pickled, stunk before we left the Place, so that we were oblig'd to throw it all away: The Men then said it was impossible to salt any Beef in those hot Countries, so as to preserve it, and would have had us given it over, and ha' gone to the Coast of New England, or New York, for Provisions; but I soon convinc'd them of the Mistake, and by only using the Caution, viz. not to salt up any Beef of those Cattle that had been hunted, we cur'd one hundred and forty Barrels of very good Beef, and such as lasted us a very great while.

I began to be of some Repute among them upon this Occasion, and Redhand took me into the Cabin with him to consult upon all Emergencies, and gave me the Name of Captain, though I had then no Command: By this Means I gave him an Account of all my Adventures in the South Seas, and what a prodigious Booty we got there with Captain Goignet, the Frenchman, and with Captain Sharp, and others; encouraging him to make an Attempt that Way, and proposing to him to go away to the Brasils, and so round by the Straits of Magellan, or Cape Horn.

However, in this he was more prudent than I, and told me, that not only the Strength but the Force of his Ship was too small, not but that he had Men enough, as he said very well, but he wanted more Guns, and a better Ship; for indeed the Ship we were in was but a weak crazy Boat for so long a Voyage: So he said he approv'd my Project very well, but that he thought we should try to take some more substantial Vessel for the Business: And says he, if we could but take a good stout Ship, fit to carry thirty Guns, and a Sloop, or Brigantine, he would go with all his Heart.

This I could not but approve of; so we form'd the Scheme of the Design, and he call'd all his Men together, and propos'd it to them, and they all approv'd it with a general Consent; and I had the Honour of being the Contriver of the Voyage. From this Time we resolv'd, some how or other, to get a better Ship under us, and it was not long before an Opportunity presented to our Mind.

Being now upon the Coast of the Island of Cuba, we stood away West, coasting the Island, and so went away for Florida, where we cruis'd among the Islands, and in the Wake of the Gulph; but nothing presented a great while; at length we spy'd a Sail, which prov'd an English homeward bound Ship from Jamaica: We immediately chac'd her, and came up with her; she was a stout Ship, and the Captain defended her very well; and had she not been a comber'd deep Ship, being full loaded, so that they could scarce come at their Guns, we should have had our Hands full of her. But when they found what we were, and that, being full of Men, we were resolv'd to be on Board them, and that we had hoisted the black Flag, a Signal that we would give them no Quarter, they began to sink in their Spirits, and soon after cry'd Quarter, offering to yield: Redhand would have given them no Quarter, but, according to his usual Practice, would have thrown the Men all into the Sea; but I prevail'd with him to give them Quarter, and good Usage too; and so they yielded; and a very rich Prize it was, only that we knew not what to do with the Cargo.

When we came to consider more seriously the Circumstances we were in by taking this Ship, and what we should do with her, we found, that she was not only deep loaden, but was a very heavy Sailer, and that, in short, she was not such a Ship as we wanted; so, upon long Debate, we resolv'd to take out of her all the Rum, the Indigo, and the Money we could come at, with about twenty Casks of Sugar, and twelve of her Guns, with all the Ammunition, small Arms, Bullets, &c. and let her go; which was accordingly done, to the great Joy of the Captain that commanded her: However, we took in her about six thousand Pounds Sterling in Pieces of Eight.

But the next Prize we met, suited us better on all Accounts, being a Ship from Kingsale in Ireland, loaden with Beef, and Butter, and Beer, for Barbadoes; never was Ship more welcome to Men in our Circumstances; this was the very Thing we wanted: We saw the Ship early in the Morning, at about five Leagues Distance, and we was three Days in Chace of her; she stood from us, as if she would have run away for the Cape de Verd Islands, and two or three Times we thought she sail'd so well she would have got away from us, but we had always the good Luck to get Sight of her in the Morning: She was about 260 Tun, an English Frigat-built Ship, and had 12 Guns on Board, but could carry 20. The Commander was a Quaker, but yet had he been equal to us in Force, it appear'd by his Countenance he would not have been afraid of his Flesh, or have baulk'd using the Carnal Weapon of Offence, viz. the Cannon Ball.

We soon made ourselves Master of this Ship when once we came up with him, and he was every Thing that we wanted; so we began to shift our Guns into her, and shifted about 60 Tun of her Butter and Beef into our own Frigate; this made the Irish Vessel be a clear Ship, lighter in the Water, and have more Room on Board for Fight, if Occasion offer'd.

When we had the old Quaking Skipper on Board, we ask'd him whether he would go along with us; he gave us no Answer at first; but when we ask'd him again, he return'd, that he did not know whether it might be safe for him to answer the Question: We told him, he should either go or stay, as he pleas'd; Why then, says he, I had rather ye will give me Leave to decline it.

We gave him Leave, and accordingly set him on Shore afterwards at Nevis, with ten of his Men; the rest went along with us as Volunteers, except the Carpenter and his Mate, and the Surgeon, those we took by Force: We were now supply'd as well as Heart could wish, had a large Ship in our Possession, with Provisions enough for a little Fleet rather than for a single Ship. So with this Purchase we went away for the Leeward Islands, and fain we would have met with some of the New York or New England Ships, which generally come loaden with Peas, Flower, Pork, &c. But it was a long while before any Thing of that Kind presented. We had promis'd the Irish Captain to set him on Shore, with his Company, at Nevis, but we were not willing till we had done our Business in those Seas, because of giving the Alarm among the Islands; so we went away for St. Domingo, and making that Island our Rendezvous, we cruis'd to the Eastward, in Hopes of some Purchase; it was not long before we spy'd a Sail, which prov'd to be a Burmoodas Sloop, but bound from Virginia or Maryland, with Flower, Tobacco, and some Malt; the last a Thing which in particular we knew not what to do with: However, the Flower and Tobacco was very welcome, and the Sloop no less welcome than the rest; for she was a very large Vessel, and carry'd near 60 Tun, and when not so deep loaden, prov'd an excellent Sailer. Soon after this we met with another Sloop, but she was bound from Barbadoes to New England, with Rum, Sugar, and Molosses: Nothing disturb'd us in taking this Vessel, but that being willing enough to let her go; (for as to the Sugar and Molosses, we had neither Use for them, or Room for them) but to have let her go, had been to give the Alarm to all the Coast of North America, and then what we wanted would never come in our Way. Our Captain, justly call'd Redhand, or Bloodyhand, was presently for dispatching them, that they might tell no Tales; and, indeed, the Necessity of the Method had very near prevail'd; nor did I much interpose here, I know not why, but some of the other Men put him in as good a Way; and that was, to bring the Sloop to an Anchor under the Lee of St. Domingo, and take away all her Sails, that she should not stir till we gave her Leave.

We met with no less than five Prizes more here in about 20 Days Cruise, but none of them for our Turn; one of them, indeed, was a Vessel bound to St. Christopher's with Madera Wine: We borrow'd about 20 Pipes of the Wine, and let her go. Another was a New England built Ship, of about 150 Tun, bound also Home with Sugar and Molosses, which was good for nothing to us; however, we gat near 1000 l. on Board her in Pieces of Eight, and taking away her Sails, as before, brought her to an Anchor under the Lee of the Sloop: At last we met with what we wanted, and this was another Ship of about 100 Tun, from New England, bound to Barbadoes; she had on Board 150 Barrels of Flower, about 350 Barrels of Pease, and 10 Tun of Pork barrell'd up and pickel'd, besides some live Hogs, and some Horses, and six Tun of Beer.

We were now sufficiently provided for; in all those Prizes we got also about 56 Men, who, by Choice and Volunteer, agree'd to go along with us, including the Carpenters and Surgeons, who we oblig'd always to go; so that we were now above 200 Men, two Ships, and the Burmoodas Sloop; and giving the other Sloop, and the New England homeward bound Ship their Sails again, we let them go; and as to the Malt which we took in the Burmoodas Sloop, we gave it the last New England Master, who was going to Barbadoes.

We gat in all those Ships, besides the Provisions above-mention'd, about 200 Musquets and Pistols, good Store of Cutlasses, about 20 Tun of Iron Shot and Musquet Ball, and 33 Barrels of good Powder, which was all very suitable Things to our Occasions.

We were fully satisfy'd, as we said to one another, now, and concluded that we would stand away to the Windward, as well as we could, towards the Coast of Africa, that we might come in the Wind's Way for the Coast of Brasil; but our Frigat (I mean that we were first shipp'd in) was yet out upon the Cruise, and not come in; so we came to an Anchor to wait for her, when, behold, the next Morning she came in with full Sail, and a Prize in Tow: She had, it seems, been farther West than her Orders, but had met with a Spanish Prize, whither bound, or from whence, I remember we did not enquire, but we found in her, besides Merchandize, which we had no Occasion for, 65000 Pieces of Eight in Silver, some Gold, and two Boxes of Pearl of a good Value; five Dutch, or rather Flemish, Seamen that were on Board her, were willing to go with us; and as to the rest of the Cargo, we let her go, only finding four of her Guns were Brass, we took them into our Ship, with seven great Jars of Powder, and some Cannon-Shot, and let her go, using the Spaniards very civilly.

This was a Piece of meer good Fortune to us, and was so encouraging as nothing could be more, for it set us up, as we may say; for now we thought we could never fail of good Fortune, and we resolv'd, one and all, directly to the South Seas.

It was about the Middle of August 1690 that we set forward, and steering E. by S. and E. S. E. for about fifteen Days, with the Winds at N. N. W. variable, we came quickly into the Trade Winds, with a good Offing, to go clear of all the Islands; and so we steer'd directly for Cape St. Augustin in the Brasils, which we made the 22nd of September.

We cruis'd some Time upon the Coast, about the Bay of All Saints, and put in once or twice for fresh Water, especially at the Island of St. John's, where we got good Store of Fish, and some Hogs, which, for fresh Provisions, was a great Relief to us: But we gat no Purchase here; for whether it was that their European Ships were just come in, or just gone out, we know not, or whether they suspected what we were, and so kept close within their Ports, but in thirteen Days that we ply'd off and on about Fernambuque, and about fourteen Days more that we spent in coasting along the Brasil Shore to the South, we met not one Ship, neither saw a Sail, except of their Fishing-Boats or small Coasters, who kept close under Shore.

We cross'd the Line here about the latter End of September, and found the Air exceeding hot and unwholsome, the Sun being in the Zenith, and the Weather very wet and rainy; so we resolv'd to stand away South, without looking for any more Purchase on that Side.

Accordingly we kept on to the South, having tolerable good Weather, and keeping the Shore all the Way in View till we came the Length of St. Julien, in the Latitude of 48 Degrees, 22 Minutes South; here we put in again, being the Beginning of November, and took in fresh Water, and spent about ten Days, refreshing ourselves, and fitting our Tackle; all which Time we liv'd upon Penguins and Seals, of which we kill'd an innumerable Number; and when we prepar'd to go, we salted up as many Penguins as we found would serve our whole Crew, to eat them twice a Week as long as they would keep.

Here we consulted together about going thro' the Straits of Magellan; but I put them quite out of Conceit of making that troublesom and fatieguing Adventure, the Straits being so hazardous, and so many Winds requir'd to pass them; and having assur'd them, that in our Return with Bat Sharp, we went away to the Latitude of 55 Degrees 30 Minutes, and then steering due East, came open with the North Seas in five Days Run, they all agreed to go that Way.

On the 20th of November we weigh'd from Port Julien, and having a fair Wind at N. E. by E. led it away merrily, till we came into the Latitude of 54, when the Wind veering more Northerly, and then to the N. W. blowing hard, we were driven into 55 Degrees and half, but lying as near as we could to the Wind, we made some Westward Way withal: The 3d of December the Wind came up South, and S. E. by S. being now just as it were at the Beginning of the Summer Solstice in that Country.

With this Wind, which blew a fresh Gale, we stood away N. N. W. and soon found ourselves in open Sea, to the West of America; upon which we haul'd away N. by E. and N. N. E. and then N. E. when on the 20th of December we made the Land, being the Coast of Chili, in the Latitude of 41 Degrees, about the Height of Baldivia; and we stood out from hence till we made the Isle of St. Juan Fernando, where we came to an Anchor, and went on Shore to get fresh Water; also some of our Men went a hunting for Goats, of which we kill'd enough to feed us all with fresh Meat for all the while we stay'd here, which was 22 Days. [Jan. 11.]

During this Stay we sent the Sloop out to Cruise, but she came back without seeing any Vessel; after which we order'd her out again more to the North, but she was scarce gone a League, when she made a Signal that she saw a Sail, and that we should come out to help them; accordingly the Frigat put to Sea after them, but making no Signal for us to follow, we lay still, and work'd hard at cleaning our Ship, shifting some of the Rigging, and the like.

We heard no more of them in three Days, which made us repent sorely that we had not gone all three together; but the third Day they came back, tho' without any Prize, as we thought, but gave us an

Account that they had chac'd a great Ship and a Bark all Night, and the next Day; that they took the Bark the Evening before, but found little in her of Value; that the great Ship ran on Shore among some Rocks, where they durst not go in after her, but that manning out their Boats, they got on Shore so soon, that the Men belonging to her durst not land; that then they threaten'd to burn the Ship as she lay, and burn them all in her, if they did not come on Shore and surrender: They offer'd to surrender, giving them their Liberty, which our Men would not promise at first; but after some Parly, and arguing on both Sides, our Men agreed thus far, that they should remain Prisoners for so long as we were in those Seas, but that as soon as we came to the Height of Panama, or if we resolv'd to return sooner, then they should be set at Liberty; and to these hard Conditions they yielded.

Our Men found in the Ship 6 Brass Guns, 200 Sacks of Meal, some Fruit, and the Value of 160000 Pieces of Eight in Gold of Chili, as good as any in the World: It was a glittering Sight, and enough to dazzle the Eyes of those that look'd on it, to see such a Quantity of Gold laid all of a Heap together, and we began to embrace one another in Congratulation of our good Fortune.

We brought the Prisoners all to the Island Fernando, where we used them very well, built little Houses for them, gave them Bread, and Meat, and every Thing they wanted; and gave them Powder and Ball to kill Goats with, which they were fully satisfy'd with, and kill'd a great many for us too.

We continu'd to Cruise [Feb. 2] hereabout, but without finding any other Prize for near three Weeks more; so we resolv'd to go up as high as Puna, the Place where I had been so lucky before; and we assur'd our Prisoners, that in about two Months we would return, and relieve them; but they chose rather to be on Board us, so we took them all in again, and kept on with an easy Sail, at a proper Distance from Land, that we might not be known, and the Alarm given; for as to the Ship which we had taken, and which was stranded among the Rocks, as we had taken all the Men out of her, the People on the Shore, when they should find her, could think no other than that she was driven on Shore by a Storm, and that all the People were drown'd, or all escap'd and gone; and there was no Doubt but that the Ship would beat to Pieces in a very few Days.

We kept, I say, at a Distance from the Shore, to prevent giving the Alarm; but it was a needless Caution, for the Country was all alarm'd on another Account, viz. about an 130 bold Buccaneers had made their Way over Land, not at the Isthmus of Darien, as usual, but from Granada, on the Lake of Nicaragua to the North of Panama, by which, tho' the Way was longer, and the Country not so practicable as at the ordinary Passage, yet they were unmolested, for they surpriz'd the Country; and whereas the Spaniards, looking for them at the old Passage, had drawn Entrenchments, planted Guns, and posted Men at the Passages of the Mountains, to intercept them and cut them off, here they met with no Spaniards, nor any other Obstruction in their Way, but coming to the South Sea had Time, undiscover'd, to build themselves Canoes and Periaguas, and did a great deal of Mischief upon the Shore, having been follow'd, among the rest, by 80 Men more, commanded by one Guilotte, a Frenchman, an old Buccaneer; so that they were now 210 Men; and they were not long at Sea before they took two Spanish Barks going from Guatimala to Panama, loaden with Meal, Coco, and other Provisions; so that now they were a Fleet of two Barks, with several Canoes, and Periaguas, but no Guns, nor any more Ammunition than every one carry'd at first at their Backs.

However, this Troop of Desperadoes had alarm'd all the Coast, and Expresses both by Sea and Land were dispatch'd, to warn the Towns on the Coast to be upon their Guard, all the way from Panama to Lima; but as they were represented to be only such Freebooters as I have said, Ships of Strength did not desist their Voyages, as they found Occasion, as we shall observe presently: We were now gotten into the Latitude of 10, 11, and 12 Degrees and a Half; but, in our overmuch Caution, had kept out so far to Sea, that we miss'd every Thing which would otherwise have fallen into our Hands; but we were better inform'd quickly, as you shall hear.

Early in the Morning, one of our Men being on the Missen-top, cry'd, A Sail, a Sail; it prov'd to be a small Vessel standing just after us; and as we understood afterwards, did so, believing that we were some of the King's Ships looking after the Buccaneers. As we understood she was a-Stern of us, we shorten'd Sail, and hung out the Spanish Colours, separating ourselves, to make him suppose we were cruising for the Buccaneers, and did not look for him; however, when we saw him come forward, but stretching in a little towards the Shore, we took Care to be so much to Starboard that he could not escape us that Way; and when he was a little nearer, the Sloop plainly chac'd him, and in a little Time came up with him, and took him: We had little Goods in the Vessel, their chief Loading being Meal and Corn for Panama, but the Master happen'd to have 6000 Pieces of Eight in his Cabin, which was good Booty.

But that which was better than all this to us was, that the Master gave us an Account of two Ships which were behind, and were under Sail for Lima or Panama; the one having the Revenues of the Kingdom of Chili, and the other having a great Quantity of Silver, going from Puna to Lima, to be forwarded from thence to Panama, and that they kept together, being Ships of Force, to protect one another; how they did it we soon saw the Effects of.

Upon this Intelligence we were very joyful, and assur'd the Master, that if we found it so, we would give him his Vessel again, and all his Goods, except his Money, as for That, we told him, such People as we never return'd it any Body: However, the Man's Intelligence prov'd good, for the very next Day, as we were standing South-West, our Spanish Colours being out, as above, we spy'd one of the Ships, and soon after the other; we found they had discover'd us also, and that being doubtful what to make of us, they tack'd and stood Eastward to get nearer the Land; we did the like, and as we found there was no letting them go that Way but that we should be sure to lose them, we soon let them know that we were resolv'd to speak with them.

The biggest Ship, which was three Leagues a-Stern of the other, crowded in for the Shore with all the Sail, she could make, and it was easy for us to see that she would escape us; for as she was a great deal farther in with the Land than the other when we first gave Chace, so in about three Hours we saw the Land plain a-Head of us, and that the great Ship would get into Port before we could reach her.

Upon this we stretch'd a-Head with all the Sail we could make, and the Sloop, which crowded also very hard, and out-went us, engag'd the small Ship at least an Hour before we could come up: But she could make little of it, for the Spanish Ship having 12 Guns and 6 Patereroes, would have been too many for the Sloop if we had not come up: However, at length, our biggest Ship came up also, and, running up under her Quarter, gave her our whole Broadside; at which she struck immediately, and the Spaniards cry'd, Quarter, and Miserecordia; Upon this, our Sloop's Men enter'd her presently, and secur'd her.

In the Beginning oft his Action, it seems, our Redhand Captain was so provok'd at losing the greater Prize, which, as he thought, had all the Money on Board, that he swore he would not spare one of the Dogs, (so he call'd the Spaniards in the other Ship) but he was prevented; and it was very happy for the Spaniards, that the first Shot the Ship made towards us, just as we were running up to pour in our Broadside, I say, the first Shot took Captain Redhand full on the Breast, and shot his Head and one Shoulder off, so that he never spoke more, nor did I find that any one Man in the Ship shew'd the least Concern for him; so certain it is, that Cruelty never recommends any Man among Englishmen; no, tho' they have no Share in the suffering under it; but one said, D—n him, let him go, he was a butcherly Dog; another said, D—n him, he was a merciless Son of a B—ch; another said, he was a barbarous Dog, and the like.

But to return to the Prize, being now as certain of the smaller Prize as that we had miss'd the great one, we began to examine what we had got; and it is not easy to give an exact Account of the prodigious Variety of Things we found: In the first Place, were 116 Chests of Pieces of Eight in Specie, 72 Bars of Silver, 15 Bags of wrought Plate, which a Fryer that was on Board would have perswaded us, for the Sake of the Blessed Virgin, to have return'd, being, as he said, consecrated Plate to the Honour of the holy Church, the Virgin Mary, and St. Martin; but, as it happen'd, he could not perswade us to it; also we found about 60000 Ounces of Gold, some in little Wedges, some in Dust. We found several other Things of Value, but not to be nam'd with the rest.

Being thus made surprisingly rich, we began to think what Course we should steer next; for as the great Ship, which was escap'd, would certainly alarm the Country, we might be sure we should meet with no more Purchase at Sea, and we were not very fond of landing, to attack any Town on Shore. In this Consultation 'tis to be observ'd, that I was, by the unanimous Consent of all the Crew, made Captain of the great Ship, and of the whole Crew; the whole Voyage hither, and every Part of it, having, for some Time before, been chiefly manag'd by my Direction, or at least by my Advice.

The first Thing I propos'd to them all, was, seeing we had met with such good Luck, and that we could not expect much more, and if we stay'd longer in these Seas, should find it very hard to revictual our Ships, and might have our Retreat cut off by Spanish Men of war; (five of which we heard were sent out after the other Buccaneers) we should make the best of our Way to the South, and get about into the North Seas, where we were out of all Danger.

In Consequence of this Advice, which was generally approv'd, we stood away directly South; and the Wind blowing pretty fair at N. N. E. a merry Gale, we stood directly for the Isle of Juan Fernando, carrying our rich Prize with us.

We arriv'd here the Beginning of June, having been just six Months in those Seas. We were surpriz'd, when coming to the Island, we found two Ships at an Anchor close under the Lee of the Rocks, and two little Periaguas farther in, near the Shore; but being resolv'd to see what they were, we found, to our Satisfaction, they were the Buccaneers of whom I have spoken above: The Story is too long to enter upon here; but in short, without Guns, without Ship, and only coming over Land with their Fusees in their Hands, they had rang'd these Seas, had taken several Prizes, and some pretty rich, and had got two pretty handsome Barks, one carry'd six Guns, and the other four; they had shar'd, as they told us, about 400 Pieces of Eight a Man, besides one Thing they had which we were willing to buy of them; they had about 100 Jarrs of Gunpowder, which they took out of a Store Ship going to Lima.

If we was glad to meet them, you may be sure they were glad to meet with us, and so we began to sort together as one Company, only they were loth to give over and return, as we were and which we had now resolv'd on.

We were so rich ourselves, and so fully satisfy'd with what we had taken, that we began to be bountiful to our Countrymen; and indeed they dealt so generously with us, that we could not but be inclin'd to do them some Good, for when we talk'd of buying their Gunpowder, they very frankly gave us 50 Jarrs of it gratis.

I took this so kindly, that I call'd a little Council among ourselves, and propos'd to send the poor Rogues 50 Barrels of our Beef, which we could very well spare; and our Company agreeing to it, we did so, which made their Hearts glad; for it was very good, and they had not tasted good Salt-beef for a long Time; and with it we sent them two Hogsheads of Rum: This made them so hearty to us, that they sent two of their Company to compliment us, to offer to enter themselves on Board us, and to go with us all the World over.

We did not so readily agree to this at first, because we had no new Enterprize in View; but however, as they sent us Word they had chosen me so unanimously for their Captain, I propos'd to our Men to remove ourselves, and all our Goods, into the great Ship and the Sloop, and so take the honest Fellows into the Fregat, which now had no less than 22 Guns, and would hold them all, and then they might sail with us, or go upon any Adventures of their own, as we should agree.

Accordingly we did so, and gave them that Ship, with all her Guns and Ammunition, but made one of our own Men Captain, which they consented to, and so we became all one Body.

Here also we shar'd our Booty, which was great indeed to a Profusion; and as keeping such a Treasure in every Man's particular private Possession, would have occasion'd Gaming, Quarrelling, and perhaps Thieving and Pilfering, I order'd that so many small Chests should be made as there were Men in the Ship, and every Man's Treasure was nail'd up in these Chests, and the Chests all stow'd in the Hold, with every Man's Name upon his Chest, not to be touch'd but by general Order, and to prevent Gaming, I prevail'd with them to make a Law or Agreement, and everyone to set their Hands to it; by which they agreed, That if any Man play'd for any more Money than he had in his Keeping, the Winner should not be paid whatever the Loser run in Debt, but the Chest containing every Man's Dividend, should be all his own, to be deliver'd whole to him; and the Offender, whenever he left the Ship, if he would pay any Gaming Debts afterward, that was another Case; but such Debts should never be paid while he continu'd in that Company.

By this Means also we secur'd the Ship's Crew keeping together; for if any Man left the Ship now, he was sure to leave about 6000 Pieces of Eight behind him, to be shar'd among the rest of the Ship's Company, which few of them car'd to do.

As we were now all embark'd together, the next Question was, Whither we should go? As for our Crew, we were so rich, that our Men were all for going back again, and so to make off to some of the Leeward Islands, that we might get a-Shore privately with our Booty: But as we had shipp'd our new Comrades on Board a good Ship, it would be very hard to oblige them to go back without any Purchace, for that would be to give them a Ship to do them no Good, but to carry them back to Europe just as they came out from thence, viz. with no Money in their Pockets.

Upon these Considerations we came to this Resolution, That they should go out to Sea and Cruise the Height of Lima, and try their Fortune, and that we would stay 60 Days for them at Juan Fernando.

Upon this Agreement they went away very joyful, and we fell to work to new rig our Ship, mending our Sails, and cleaning our Bottom. Here we employ'd ourselves a Month very hard at Work; our Carpenters also took down some of the Ship's upper Work, and built it, as we thought, more to the Advantage of Sailing; so that we had more Room within, and yet did not lie so high.

During this Time we had a Tent set up on Shore, and 50 of our Men employ'd themselves wholly in killing Goats and Fowls for our fresh Provisions; and one of our Men understanding we had some Malt left on Board the Ship, which was taken in one of the Prizes, set up a great Kettle on Shore, and went to work to Brewing, and, to our great Satisfaction, brew'd us some very good Beer; but we wanted Bottles to keep it in, after it had stood a while in the Cask.

However, he brew'd us very good Small Beer, for present Use; and instead of Hops he found some wild Wormwood growing on the Island, which gave it no unpleasant Taste, and made it very agreeable to us.

Before the Time was expir'd, our Frigat sent a Sloop to us, which they had taken, to give us Notice that they were in a small Creek near the Mould of the River Guyaquil, on the Coast of Peru, in the Latitude of 22 Degrees. They had a great Booty in View, there being two Ships in the River of Guyaquil, and two more expected to pass by from Lima, in which was a great Quantity of Plate; that they waited there for them, and begg'd we would not think the Time long; but that if we should go away, they desir'd that we would fix up a Post, with a Piece of Lead on it, signifying where they should come to us, and wherever it was, East or West, North or South, they would follow us with all the Sail they could make.

A little while after this, they sent another Sloop, which they had taken also; and she brought a vast Treasure in Silver and very rich Goods, which they had got in plundering a Town on the Continent; and they order'd the Sloop to wait for them at the Island where we lay, till their Return: But they were so eager in the Pursuit of their Game, that they could not think of coming back yet, neither could we blame them, they having such great Things in View: So we resolv'd, in Pursuit of our former Resolution, to be gone; and after several Consultations among our selves in what Part of the World we should pitch our Tent, we broke up at first without any Conclusion.

We were all of the Opinion, that our Treasure was so great, that wherever we went, we should be a Prey to the Government of that Place; that it was impossible to go all on Shore, and be conceal'd; and that we should be so jealous of one another, that we should certainly betray one another, everyone for fear of his Fellow, that is to say, for fear the other should tell first. Some therefore propos'd our going about the South Point of Cape Horne, and that then, going away to the Gulph of Mexico, we should go on Shore at the Bay of Campeachy, and from thence disperse ourselves as well as we could, and every one go his own Way.

I was willing enough to have gone thither, because of the Treasure I had left there under Ground; but still I concluded we were (as I have said) too rich to go on Shore any where to separate, for every Man of us had too much Wealth to carry about us; and if we separated, the first Number of Men any of us should meet with, that were strong enough to do it, would take it from us, and so we should but just expose ourselves to be murder'd for that Money we had gotten at so much Hazard.

Some propos'd then our going to the Coast of Virgina, and go some on Shore in one Place, and some in another privately, and so travelling to the Sea-Ports where there were most People, we might be conceal'd, and by Degrees reduce our selves to a private Capacity, every one shifting Home as well as they could. This I acknowledge might be done, if we were sure none of us would be false one to another; but while Tales might be told, and the Teller of the Tale was sure to save his own Life and Treasure, and make his Peace at the Expence of his Comrade's, there was no Safety; and they might be sure, that as the Money would render them suspected wherever they came, so they would be examin'd, and what by faltering in their Story, and by being cross-examin'd, kept apart, and the one being made to believe the other had betray'd him, and told all, when indeed he might have said nothing to hurt him, the Truth of Fact would be dragg'd out by Piece-meal, till they would certainly at last come to the Gallows.

These Objections were equally just, to what Nation or Place soever we could think of going: So that upon the whole, we concluded there was no Safety for us but by keeping all together, and going to some Part of the World where we might be strong enough to defend ourselves, or be so conceal'd till we might find out some Way of Escape that we might not now be so well able to think of.

In the Middle of all these Consultations, in which I freely own I was at a Loss, and could not tell which Way to advise, an old Sailor stood up, and told us, if we would be advis'd by him, there was a Part of the World where he had been, where we might all settle ourselves undisturb'd, and live very comfortably and plentifully, till we could find out some Way how to dispose of ourselves better; and that we might easily be strong enough for the Inhabitants, who would at first, perhaps, attack us, but that afterwards they would sort very well with us, and supply us with all Sorts of Provisions very plentifully; and this was the Island of Madagascar: He told us we might live very well there. He gave us a large Account of the Country, the Climate, the People, the Plenty of Provisions which was to be had there, especially of black Cattle, of which, he said, there was an infinite Number, and consequently a Plenty of Milk, of which so many other Things was made: In a Word, he read us so many Lectures upon the Goodness of the Place, and the Conveniency of living there, that we were, one and all, eager to go thither, and concluded upon it.

Accordingly, having little left to do, (for we had been in a sailing Posture some Weeks) we left word with the Officer who commanded the Sloop, and with all his Men, that they should come after us to Madagascar; and our Men were not wanting to let them know all our Reasons for going thither, as well as the Difficulties we found of going any where else, which had so fully possess'd them with the Hopes of farther Advantage, that they promis'd for the rest that they would all follow us.

However, as we all calculated the Length of the Voyage, and that our Water, and perhaps our Provisions might not hold out so far, but especially our Water, we agreed, that having pass'd Cape Horn, and got into the North Seas, we would steer Northward up the East Shore of America till we came to St. Julien, where we would stay at least fourteen Days to take in Water, and to store ourselves with Seals and Penguins, which would greatly eek out our Ship's Stores; and that then we should cross the great Atlantick Ocean in a milder Latitude than if we went directly, and stood immediately over from the Passage about the Cape, which must be, at least, in 55 or 56, and perhaps, as the Weather might be, would be in the Latitude of 60 or 61.

With this Resolution, and under these Measures, we set Sail from the Island of St. Juan Fernando the 23d of September, (being the same there as our March is here) and keeping the Coast of Chili on Board, had good Weather for about a Fortnight, [Octob. 14.] till we came into the Latitude of 44 Degrees South; when finding the Wind come squally off the Shore from among the Mountains, we were oblig'd to keep farther out at Sea, where the Winds were less uncertain; and some Calms we met with, till about the Middle of October, [16.] when the Wind springing up at N. N. W. a pretty moderate Gale, we jogg'd S. E. and S. S. E. till we came into the Latitude of 55 Degrees; and the 16th of November, found our selves in 59 Degrees, the Weather exceeding cold and severe. But the Wind holding fair, we held in with the Land, and steering E. S. E. we held that Course till we thought ourselves entirely clear of the Land, and enter'd into the North Sea, or Atlantick Ocean; and then changing our Course, we steer'd N. and N. N. E. but the Wind blowing still at N. N. W. a pretty stiff Gale, we could make nothing of it till we made the Land in the Latitude of 52 Degrees; and when we came close under Shore, we found the Winds variable; so we made still N. under the Lee of the Shore, and made the Point of St. Julien the 13th of November, having been a Year and seven Days since we parted from thence on our Voyage Outwardbound.

Here we rested ourselves, took in fresh Water, and began to kill Seals and Fowls of several Sorts, but especially Penguins, which this Place is noted for; and here we stay'd, in Hopes our Fregate would arrive, but we heard no News of her; so, at Parting, we set up a Post, with this Inscription, done on a Plate of Lead, with our Names upon the Lead, and these Words;

Gone to Madagascar, December 10, 1692.

(Being in that Latitude the longest Day in the Year;) and I doubt not but the Post may stand there still.

From hence we launch'd out into the vast Atlantick Ocean, steering our Coast E. by N. and E. N. E. till we had sail'd, by our Account, about 470 Leagues, taking our Meridian Distance, or Departure, from St. Julian. And here a strong Gale springing up at S. E. by E. and E. S. E. encreasing afterwards to a violent Storm, we were forc'd by it to the Norward, as high as the Tropick; not that it blew a Storm all the while, but it blew so steady, and so very hard, for near 20 Days together, that we were carry'd quite out of our intended Course: After we had weather'd this, we began to recover ourselves again, making still East; and endeavouring to get to the Southward, we had yet another hard Gale of Wind at S. and S. S. E. so strong, that we could make nothing of it at all; whereupon it was resolv'd, if we could, to make the Island of St. Helena, which in about three Weeks more we very happily came to, on the 17th of January.

It was to our great Satisfaction that we found no Ships at all here, and we resolv'd not by any Means to let the Governor on Shore know our Ship's Name, or any of our Officers Names; and I believe our Men were very true to one another in that Point, but they were not at all shy of letting them know upon what Account we were, &c. so that if he could have gotten any of us in his Power, as we were afterwards told he endeavour'd by two or three Ambuscades to do, we should have pass'd our Time but very indifferently; for which, when we went away, we let him know we would not have fail'd to have beat his little Port about his Ears.

We stay'd no longer here than just serv'd to refresh ourselves, and supply our Want of fresh Water; the Wind presenting fair, Feb. 2. 1692, we set Sail, and (not to trouble my Story with the Particulars of the Voyage, in which nothing remarkable occur'd) we doubled the Cape the 13th of March, and passing on without coming to an Anchor, or discovering ourselves, we made directly to the Island of Madagascar, where we arriv'd the 7th of April; the Sloop, to our particular Satisfaction, keeping in Company all the Way, and bearing the Sea as well as our Ship upon all Occasions.

To this Time I had met with nothing but good Fortune; Success answer'd every Attempt, and follow'd every Undertaking, and we scarce knew what it was to be disappointed; but we had an Interval of our Fortunes to meet with in this Place: We arriv'd, as above, at the Island on the 13th of March, but we did not care to make the South Part of the Island our Retreat; nor was it a proper Place for our Business, which was to take Possession of a private secure Place to make a Refuge of: So after staying some Time where we put in, which was on the Point of Land a little to the South of Cape St. Augustine, and taking in Water and Provisions there, we stood away to the North, and keeping the Island in View, went on till we came to the Latitude of 14 Degrees: Here we met with a very terrible Tornado, or Hurricane, which, after we had beat the Sea as long as we could, oblig'd us to run directly for the Shore to save our Lives as well as we could, in Hopes of finding some Harbour or Bay where we might run in, or at least might go into smooth Water till the Storm was over.

The Sloop was more put to it than we were in the great Ship, and being oblig'd to run afore it, a little sooner than we did, she serv'd for a Pilot-Boat to us which follow'd; in a Word, she run in under the Lee of a great Head-land, which jetted far out into the Sea, and stood very high also, and came to an Anchor in three Fathom and a half Water: We follow'd her, but not with the same good Luck, tho' we came to an Anchor too, as we thought, safe enough; but the Sea going very high, our Anchor came Home in the Night, and we drove on Shore in the Dark among the Rocks, in spight of all we were able to do.

Thus we lost the most fortunate Ship that ever Man sail'd with; however, making Signals of Distress to the Sloop, and by the Assistance of our own Boat, we sav'd our Lives; and the Storm abating in the Morning, we had Time to save many Things, particularly our Guns, and most of our Ammunition; and, which was more than all the rest, we sav'd our Treasure: Tho' I mention the saving our Guns first, yet they were the last Things we sav'd, being oblig'd to break the upper Deck of the Ship up for them.

Being thus got on Shore, and having built us some Huts for our Conveniency, we had nothing before us but a View of fixing our Habitations in the Country; for tho' we had the Sloop, we could propose little Advantage by her; for as to cruising for Booty among the Arabians or Indians, we had neither Room, for it or Inclination to it; and as for attacking any European Ship, the Sloop was in no Condition to do it, tho' we had all been on Board; for every Body knows that all the Ships trading from Europe to the East-Indies, were Ships of Force, and too strong for us; so that, in short, we had nothing in View for several Months but how to settle ourselves here, and live as comfortably and as well as we could, till something or other might offer for our Deliverance.

In this Condition we remain'd on Shore above eight Months, during which Time we built us a little Town, and fortify'd it by the Direction of one of our Gunners, who was a very good Engineer, in a very clever and regular Manner, placing a very strong double Palisado round the Foot of our Works, and a very large Ditch without our Palisado, and a third Palisado beyond the Ditch, like a Counterscarp or Cover'd-way; besides this, we rais'd a large Battery next to the Sea, with a Line of 24 Guns plac'd before it, and thus we thought ourselves in a Condition to defend ourselves against any Force that could attempt us in that Part of the World.

And besides all this, the Place on which our Habitation was built, being an Island, there was no coming easily at us by Land.

But I was far from being easy in this Situation of our Affairs; so I made a Proposal to our Men one Day, that tho' we were well enough in our Habitation, and wanted for nothing, yet since we had a Sloop here, and a Boat so good as she was, 'twas Pity she should lye and perish there, but we should send her Abroad, and see what might happen; that perhaps it might be our good Luck to surprise some Ship or other for our Turn, and so we might all go to Sea again: The Proposal was well enough relish'd at first Word, but the great Mischief of all was like to be this, That we should all go together by the Ears upon the Question who should go in her: My secret Design was laid, that I was resolv'd to go in her myself, and that she should not go without me; but when it began to be talk'd of, I discover'd the greatest seeming Resolution not to stir, but to stay with the rest, and take Care of the main Chance, that was to say, the Money.

I found, when they saw that I did not propose to go myself, the Men were much the easier; for at first they began to think it was only a Project of mine to run away from them; and so indeed it was: However, as I did not at first propose to go my self, so when I came to the Proposal of who should go, I made a long Discourse to them of the Obligation they had all to be faithful one to another, and that those who went in the Sloop, ought to consider themselves and those that were with them to be but one Body with those who were left behind; that their whole Concern ought to be to get some good Ship to fetch them off: At last, I concluded, with a Proposal, that who ever went in the Sloop, should leave his Money behind in the common Keeping, as it was before; to remain as a Pledge for his faithful performing the Voyage, and coming back again to the Company; and should faithfully swear that wherever they went, (for as to the Voyage, they were at full Liberty to go whither they would) they would certainly endeavour to get back to Madagascar; and that if they were cast away, stranded, taken, or whatever befel them, they should never rest till they got to Madagascar, if it was possible.

They all came most readily into this Proposal, for those who should go into the Sloop, but with this Alteration in them, (which was easy to be seen in their Countenances) viz. that from that Minute there was no striving who should go, but every Man was willing to stay where they were: This was what I wanted, and I let it rest for two or three Days; when I took Occasion to tell them, that seeing they all were sensible that it was a very good Proposal to send the Sloop out to Sea, and see what they could do for us, I thought it was strange they should so generally shew themselves backward to the Service for fear of parting from their Money; I told them that no Man need be afraid, that the whole Body should agree to take his Money from him without any pretended Offence, much less when he should be Abroad for their Service: But however, as it was my Proposal, and I was always willing to hazard myself for the Good of them all, so I was ready to go on the Conditions I had propos'd to them for others, and I was not afraid to flatter myself with serving them so well Abroad, that they should not grudge to restore me my Share of Money when I came Home, and the like of all those that went with me.

This was so seasonably spoken, and humour'd so well, that it answer'd my Design effectually, and I was voted to go nemine contradicente; then I desir'd they would either draw Lots for who and who should go with me, or leave it in my absolute Choice to pick and cull my Men: They had for some Time agreed to the first; and forty Blanks were made for those to whose Lot it should come to draw a Blank to go in the Sloop; but then it was said, this might neither be a fair nor an effectual Choice; for Example, if the needful Number of Officers, and of particular Occupations, should not happen to be lotted out, the Sloop might be oblig'd to go out to Sea without a Surgeon, or without a Carpenter, or without a Cook, and the like: So, upon second Thoughts, it was left to me to name my Men; so I chose me out forty stout Fellows, and among them several who were trusty bold Men, fit for any thing.

Being thus Mann'd, the Sloop rigg'd, and having clear'd her Bottom, and laid in Provisions enough for a long Voyage, we set Sail the 3d of January 1694, for the Cape of Good Hope. We very honestly left our Money, as I said, behind us, only that we had about the Value of 2000 Pound in Pieces of Eight allow'd us on Board for any Exigence that might happen at Sea.

We made no Stop at the Cape, or at St. Helena, tho' we pass'd in Sight of it, but stood over to the Caribbee Islands directly, and made the Island of Tobago the 18th of February, where we took in fresh Water, which we stood in great Need of, as you may judge by the Length of the Voyage. We sought no Purchase, for I had fully convinc'd our Men, that our Business was not to appear, as we were used to be, upon the Cruise, but as Traders; and to that End I propos'd to go away to the Bay of Campeachy, and load Logwood, under the Pretence of selling of which we might go any where.

It is true, I had another Design here, which was to recover the Money which my Comrade and I had bury'd there; and having the Man on Board with me to whom I had communicated my Design, we found an Opportunity to come at our Money with Privacy enough, having so conceal'd it, as that it would have lain there to the general Conflagration, if we had not come for it our selves.

My next Resolution was to go for England, only that I had too many Men, and did not know what to do with them: I told them we could never pretend to go with a Sloop loaden with Logwood to any Place, with 40 Men on Board, but we should be discover'd; but if they would resolve to put 15 or 16 Men on Shore as private Seamen, the rest might do well enough; and if they thought it hard to be set on Shore, I was content to be one, only that I thought it was very reasonable that whoever went on Shore should have some Money given them, and that all should agree to rendezvous in England, and so make the best of our Way thither, and there perhaps we might get a good Ship to go fetch off our Comrades and our Money. With this Resolution, sixteen of our Men had three hundred Pieces of Eight a Man given them, and they went off thus; the Sloop stood away North, thro' the Gulph of Florida, keeping under the Shore of Carolina and Virginia; so our Men dropp'd off as if they had deserted the Ship; three of the sixteen run away there, five more went off at Virginia, three at New York, three at Road Island, and myself and one more at New England; and so the Sloop went away for England with the rest. I got all my Money on Shore with me, and conceal'd it as well as I could; some I got Bills for, some I bought Molosses with, and turn'd the rest into Gold; and dressing myself not as a common Sailor, but as a Master of a Ketch, which I had lost in the Bay of Campeachy, I got Passage on Board one Captain Guillame, a New England Captain, whose Owner was one Mr. Johnson a Merchant, living at Hackney, near London.

Being at London, it was but a very few Months before several of us met again, as I have said we agreed to do. And being true to our first Design of going back to our Comrades, we had several close Conferences about the Manner and Figure in which we should make the Attempt, and we had some very great Difficulties appear'd in our Way: First, to have fitted up a small Vessel, it would be of no Service to us, but be the same Thing as the Sloop we came in; and if we pretended to a great Ship, our Money would not hold out; so we were quite at a Stand in our Councils what to do, or what Course to take, till at length our Money still wasting, we grew less able to execute any Thing we should project.

This made us all desperate; when as desperate Distempers call for desperate Cures, I started a Proposal which pleas'd them all, and this was, that I would endeavour among my Acquaintance, and with what Money I had left, (which was still sixteen or seventeen hundred Pound) to get the Command of a good Ship, bearing a quarter Part, or thereabout, myself; and so having gat into the Ship, and got a Freight, the rest of our Gang should all enter on Board as Seamen, and whatever Voyage we went, or wheresoever we were bound, we would run away with the Ship and all the Goods, and so go to our Friends as we had promis'd.

I made several Attempts of this Kind, and once bought a very good Ship, call'd, The Griffin, of one Snelgrove a Shipwright, and engag'd the Persons concern'd to hold a Share in her and fit her out, on a Voyage for Leghorn and Venice; when it was very probable the Cargo, to be shipp'd on Board casually by the Merchant, would be very rich; but Providence, and the good Fortune of the Owner prevented this Bargain, for without any Objection against me, or Discovery of my Design in the least, he told me afterwards his Wife had an ugly Dream or two about the Ship; once, that it was set on Fire by Lightning, and he had lost all he had in it; another Time, that the Men had mutiny'd and conspir'd to kill him; and that his Wife was so averse to his being concern'd in it, that it had always been an unlucky Ship, and that therefore his Mind was chang'd; that he would sell the whole Ship, if I would, but he would not hold any Part of it himself.

Tho' I was very much disappointed at this, yet I put a very good Face upon it, and told him, I was very glad to hear him tell me the Particulars of his Dissatisfaction; for if there was any Thing in Dreams, and his Wife's Dream had any Signification at all, it seem'd to concern me (more than him) who was to go the Voyage, and command the Ship; and whether the Ship was to be burnt, or the Men to mutiny, tho' Part of the Loss might be his, who was to stay on Shore, all the Danger was to be mine, who was to be at Sea in her; and then, as he had said, she had been an unlucky Ship to him, it was very likely she would be so to me; and therefore I thank'd him for the Discovery, and told him I would not meddle with her.

The Man was uneasy, and began to waver in his Resolution, and had it not been for the continu'd Importunities of his Wife, I believe would have come on again; for People generally encline to a Thing that is rejected, when they would reject the same Thing when profer'd: But I knew it was not my Business to let myself be blow'd upon, so I kept to my Resolution, and wholly declin'd that Affair, on Pretence of its having got an ill Name for an unlucky Ship; and that Name stuck so to her, that the Owners could never sell her, and, as I have been inform'd since, were oblig'd to break her up at last.

It was a great while I spent with hunting after a Ship, but was every Way disappointed, till Money grew short, and the Number of my Men lessen'd apace, and at last we were reduc'd to seven, when an Opportunity happen'd in my Way to go Chief-Mate on Board a stout Ship bound from London to . . . . .

[N. B. In Things so modern, it is no Way convenient to write to you particular Circumstances and Names of Persons, Ships, or Places, because those Things being in themselves criminal, may be call'd up in Question in a judicial Way; and therefore I warn the Reader to observe, that not only all the Names are omitted, but even the Scene of Action in this criminal Part, is not laid exactly as Things were acted; least I should give Justice a Clew to unravel my Story by, which no Body will blame me for avoiding.]

It is enough to tell the Reader, that being put out to Sea, and being for Conveniency of Wind and Weather come to an Anchor on the Coast of Spain, my seven Companions having resolv'd upon our Measures, and having brought three more of the Men to confederate with us, we took up Arms in the middle of the Night, secur'd the Captain, the Gunner, and the Carpenter, and after that, all the rest of the Men, and declar'd our Intention: The Captain and nine Men refus'd to come into our projected Roguery, (for we gave them their Choice to go with us, or go on Shore) so we put them on Shore very civilly, gave the Master his Books, and every Thing he could carry with him; and all the rest of the Men agreed to go along with us.

As I had resolv'd, before I went on Board, upon what I purpos'd to do, so I had laid out all the Money I had left in such Things as I knew I should want, and had caus'd one of my Men to pretend he was going to — to build or buy a Ship there, and that he wanted Freight for a great deal of Cordage, Anchors, eight Guns, Powder and Ball, with about 20 Tun of Lead and other bulky Goods, which were all put on Board as Merchandize.

We had not abundance of Bail Goods on Board, which I was glad of; not that I made any Conscience or Scruple of carrying them away, if the Ship had been full of them; but we had no Market for them: Our first Business was to get a larger Store of Provision on Board than we had, our Voyage being long; and having acquainted the Men with our Design, and promis'd the new Men a Share of the Wealth we had there, which made them very hearty to us, we set Sail: We took in some Beef and Fish, at — where we lay fifteen Days, but out of all Reach of the Castle or Fort; and having done our Business, sail'd away for the Canaries, where we took in some Butts of Wine, and some fresh Water: With the Guns the Ship had, and those eight I had put on Board as Merchandize, we had then two and thirty Guns mounted, bur were but slenderly Mann'd, tho' we gat four English Seamen at the Canaries; but we made up the Loss at Fiall, where we made bold with three English Ships we found, and partly by fair Means, and partly by Force, shipp'd twelve Men there; after which, without any farther Stop for Men or Stores, we kept the Coast of Africa on Board 'till we pass'd the Line, and then stood off to St. Helena.

Here we took in fresh Water, and some fresh Provisions, and went directly for the Cape of Good Hope, which we pass'd, stopping only to fill about 22 Butts of Water, and with a fair Gale enter'd the Sea of Madagascar, and sailing up the West Shore, between the Island and the Coast of Africa, came to an Anchor over against our Settlement, about two Leagues Distance, and made the Signal of our Arrival, with firing twice seven Guns at the Distance of a Two-Minute Glass between the Seven; when, to our infinite Joy, the Fort answer'd us, and the Long-boat, the same that belong'd to our former Ship, came off to us.

We embrac'd one another with inexpressible Joy, and the next Morning I went on Shore, and our Men brought our Ship safe into Harbour, lying within the Defence of our Platform, and within two Cables length of the Shore, good soft Ground, and in eleven Fathom Water, having been three Months and eighteen Days on the Voyage, and almost three Years absent from the Place.

When I came to look about me here, I found our Men had encreas'd their Number, and that a Vessel which had been cruising, that is to say, Pirating on the Coast of Arabia, having seven Dutchmen, three Portuguese, and five Englishmen on Board, had been cast away upon the Northern Shore of that Island, and had been taken up and reliev'd by our Men, and liv'd among them. They told us also of another Crew of European Sailors, which lay, as we did, on the Main of the Island, and had lost their Ship and were, as the Islanders told them, above a hundred Men, but we heard nothing who they were.

Some of our Men were dead in the mean Time, I think about three; and the first Thing I did was to call a Muster, and see how Things stood as to Money: I found the Men had been very true to one another; there lay all the Money, in Chests piled up as I left it, and every Man's Money having his Name upon it: Then acquainting the rest with the Promise I had made the Men that came with me, they all agreed to it; so the Money belonging to the dead Men, and to the rest of the forty Men who belong'd to the Sloop, was divided among the Men I brought with me, as well those who join'd at first, as those we took in at the Cape de Verd, and the Canaries: And the Bails of Goods which we found in the Ship, many of which were valuable for our own Use, we agreed to give them all to the fifteen Men mention'd above, who had been sav'd by our Men, and so to buy what we wanted of those Goods of them, which made their Hearts glad also.

And now we began to consult what Course to take in the World: As for going to England, tho' our Men had a great Mind to be there, yet none of them knew how to get thither, notwithstanding I had brought them a Ship; but I, who had now made myself too publick to think any more of England, had given over all Views that Way, and began to cast about for farther Adventures; for tho', as I said, we were immensely rich before, yet I abhorr'd lying still, and burying my self alive, as I call'd it, among Savages and Barbarians; besides, some of our Men were young in the Trade, and had seen nothing; and they lay at me every Day not to lie still in a Part of the World where, as they said, such vast Riches might be gain'd; and that the Dutchmen and Englishmen who were cast away, as above, and who our Men call'd the Comelings, were continually buzzing in my Ears what infinite Wealth was to be got, if I would but make one voyage to the Coast of Malabar, Coromandel, and the Bay of Bengale; nay, the three Portuguese Seamen offer'd themselves to attack and bring off one of their biggest Galleons, even out of the Road of Goa, on the Malabar Coast, the Capital of the Portuguese Factories in the Indies.

In a Word, I was overcome with these new Proposals, and told the rest of my People, I was resolv'd to go to Sea again, and try my good Fortune; I was sorry I had not another Ship or two, but if ever it lay in my Power to master a good Ship, I would not fail to bring her to them.

While I was thus fitting out upon this new Undertaking, and the Ship lay ready to Sail, and all the Men who were design'd for the Voyage, were on Board, being 85 in Number; among which were all the Men I brought with me, the 15 Comelings, and the rest made up out of our old Number; I say, when I was just upon the Point of setting Sail, we were all surpriz'd just in the Grey of the Morning to spy a Sail at Sea; we knew not what to make of her, but found she was an European Ship; that she was not a very large Vessel, yet that she was a Ship of Force too: She seem'd to shorten Sail, as if she look'd out for some Harbour; at first Sight I thought she was English; immediately I resolv'd to slip Anchor and Cable and go out to Sea and speak with her, if I could, let her be what she would: As soon as I was got a little clear of the Land, I fir'd a Gun, and spread English Colours: She immediately brought too, fir'd three Guns, and mann'd out her Boat with a Flag of Truce: I did the like, and the two Boats spoke to one another in about two Hours, when, to our infinite Joy, we found they were our Comrades who we left in the South Seas, and to whom we gave the Fregate at the Isle of Juan Fernando.

Nothing of this Kind could have happen'd more to our mutual Satisfaction, for tho' we had long ago given them over either for Lost, or Lost to us; and we had no great Need of Company, yet we were overjoy'd at meeting, and so were they too.

They were in some Distress for Provisions, and we had Plenty; so we brought their Ship in for them, gave them a present Supply, and when we had help'd them to moor and secure the Ship in the Harbour, we made them lock all their Hatches and Cabins up, and come on Shore, and there we feasted them five or six Days, for we had a Plenty of all Sorts of Provisions, not to be exhausted; and if we had wanted an hundred Head of fat Bullocks, we could have had them for asking for of the Natives, who treated us all along with all possible Courtesy and Freedom in their Way.

The History of the Adventures and Success of these Men, from the Time we left them to the Time of their Arrival at our new Plantation, was our whole Entertainment for some Days. I cannot pretend to give the Particulars by my Memory; but as they came to us Thieves, they improv'd in their Calling to a great Degree, and, next to ourselves, had the greatest Success of any of the Buccaneers whose Story has ever been made publick.

I shall not take upon me to vouch the whole Account of their Actions, neither will this Letter contain a full History of their Adventures; but if the Account which they gave us was true, you may take it thus:

First, that having met with good Success after they left us, and having taken some extraordinary Purchase, as well in some Vessels they took at Sea, as in the Plunder of some Towns on the Shore near Guyaquil, as I have already told you, they got Information of a large Ship which was loading the King's Money at Puna, and had Orders to sail with it to Lima, in order to its being carry'd from thence to Panama by the Fleet, under the Convoy of the Flotilla, or Squadron of Men of War, which the King's Governor at Panama had sent to prevent their being insulted by the Pirates, which they had Intelligence were on the Coast; by which, we suppose, they meant us who were gone, for they could have no Notion of these Men then.

Upon this Intelligence they cruis'd off and on upon the Coast for near a Month, keeping always to the Southward of Lima, because they would not fall in the Way of the said Flotilla, and so be overpower'd and miss of their Prize: At last they met with what they look'd for, that is to say, they met with the great Ship abovenam'd: But to their great Misfortune and Disappointment, (as they first thought it to be) she had with her a Man of War for her Convoy, and two other Merchant Ships in her Company.

The Buccaneers had with them the Sloop which they first sent to us for our Intelligence, and which they made a little Fregate of, carrying eight Guns, and some Patareroes: They had not long Time to consult, but in short they resolv'd to double man the Sloop, and let her attack the great Merchant-Ship, while the Fregate, which was the whole of their Fleet, held the Man of War in Play, or at least kept him from assisting her.

According to this Resolution, they put 50 Men on Board the Sloop, which was, in short, almost as many as would stand upon her Deck one by another; and with this Force they attack'd the great Merchant-Ship, which, besides its being well mann'd, had 16 good Guns, and about 30 Men on Board. While the Sloop thus began the unequal Fight, the Man of War bore down upon her to succour the Ship under her Convoy, but the Fregate thrusting in between, engag'd the Man of War, and began a very warm Fight with her, for the Man of War had both more Guns and more Men than the Fregate after she had parted with 50 Men on Board the Sloop: While the two Men of War, as we may now call them, were thus engag'd, the Sloop was in great Danger of being worsted by the Merchant-Ship, for the Force was too much for her, the Ship was great, and her Men fought a desperate and close Fight: Twice the Sloop-Men enter'd her, and were beaten off, and about nine of their Men kill'd, several other wounded, and an unlucky Shot taking the Sloop between Wind and Water, she was oblig'd to fall a-Stern, and heel her over to stop the Leek; during which the Spaniards steer'd away to assist the Man of War, and pour'd her Broadside in upon the Fregate, which tho' but small, yet at a Time when she lay Yard-arm and Yard-arm close by the Side of the Spanish Man of War, was a great Extremity; however, the Fregate return'd her Broadside, and therewith made her sheer off, and, which was worse, shot her Main-mast thro', tho' it did not come presently by the Board.

During this Time, the Sloop having many Hands, had stopp'd the Leak, was brought to rights again, and came up again to the Engagement, and at the first Broadside had the good Luck to bring the Ship's Foremast by the Board, and thereby disabled her; but could not for all that lay her athwart, or carry her by Boarding, so that the Case began to be very doubtful; at which, the Captain of the Sloop, finding the Merchant Ship was disabled, and could not get away from them, resolv'd to leave her a while and assist the Fregate; which he did, and running a Longside our Fregate, he fairly laid the Man of War on Board just thwart his Hawser; and besides firing into her with his great Shot, he very fairly set her on Fire; and it was a great Chance but that they had been all three burnt together, but our Men helpt the Spaniards themselves to put out the Fire, and after some Time master'd it: But the Spaniards were in such a terrible Fright at the Apprehension of the Fire, that they made little Resistance afterwards, and in short, in about an Hour's Fight more, the Spanish Man of War struck, and was taken; and after that the Merchant Ship also, with all the Wealth that was in her: And thus their Victory was as compleat as it was unexpected.

The Captain of the Spanish Man of War was kill'd in the Fight, and about 36 of his Men, and most of the rest wounded, which it seems happen'd upon the Sloop's lying athwart her. This Man of War was a new Ship, and with some Alteration in her upper Work, made a very good Fregate for them, and they afterwards quitted their own Ship, and went all on Board the Spanish Ship, taking out the Main-mast of their own Ship, and making a new Fore-mast for the Spanish Ship, because her Fore-mast was also weaken'd with some Shot in her; this, however, cost them a great deal of Labour and Difficulty, and also some Time, when they came to a certain Creek, where they all went on Shore, and refresh'd themselves a while.

But if the taking the Man of War was an unexpected Victory to them, the Wealth of the Prize was much more so; for they found an amazing Treasure on Board her, both in Silver and Gold; and the Account they gave me was but imperfect, but I think they calculated the Pieces of Eight to be about 13 Tun in Weight, besides that they had 5 small Chests of Gold, some Emeralds, and, in a Word, a prodigious Booty.

They were not, however, so modest in their Prosperity as we were; for they never knew when to have done, but they must Cruise again to the Northward for more Booty, when to their great Surprize, they fell in with the Flotilla or Squadron of Men of War, which they had so studiously avoided before, and were so surrounded by them, that there was no Remedy but they must fight, and that in a Kind of Desperation, having no Prospect now but to sell their Lives as dear as they could.

This unlucky Accident befel them before they had chang'd their ship, so that they had now the Sloop and both the Men of War in Company, but they were but thinly mann'd; and as for the Booty, the greater Part of it was on Board the Sloop, that is to say, all the Gold and Emeralds, and near half the Silver.

When they saw the Necessity of fighting, they order'd the Sloop, if possible, to keep to Windward, that so she might as Night come on, make the best of her Way, and escape; but a Spanish Fregate of 18 Guns tended her so close, and sail'd so well, that the Sloop could by no Means get away from the rest; so she made up close to the Buccaneers Fregate, and maintain'd a Fight as well as she could, till in the Dusk of the Evening the Spaniards boarded and took her, but most of her Men gat away in her Boat, and some by swimming on Board the other Ship: They only left in her five wounded Englishmen, and six Spanish Negroes. The five English the barbarous Spaniards hang'd up immediately, wounded as they were.

This was good Notice to the other Men to tell them what they were to expect, and made them fight like desperate Men till Night, and kill'd the Spaniards a great many Men. It prov'd a very dark rainy Night, so that the Spaniards were oblig'd by Necessity to give over the Fight till the next Day, endeavouring, in the mean time, to keep as near them as they could: But the Buccaneers concerting their Measures where they should meet, resolv'd to make Use of the Darkness of the Night to get off if they could; and the Wind springing up a fresh Gale at S. S. W. they chang'd their Course, and, with all the Sail they could make, stood away to the N. N. W. slanting it to Seawards as nigh the Wind as they could; and getting clear away from the Spaniards, who they never saw more, they made no Stay till they pass'd the Line, and arriv'd in about 22 Days Sail on the Coast of California, where they were quite out of the Way of all Enquiry and Search of the Spaniards.

Here it was they chang'd their Ship, as I said, and quitting their own Vessel, they went all on Board the Spanish Man of War, fitting up her Masts and Rigging, as I have said, and taking out all the Guns, Stores, &c. of their own Ship, so that they had now a stout Ship under them, carrying 40 Guns, (for so many they made her carry) and well furnish'd with all Things; and tho' they had lost so great a Part of their Booty, yet they had still left a vast Wealth, being six or seven Tun of Silver, besides what they had gotten before.

With this Booty, and regretting heartily they had not practis'd the same Moderation before, they resolv'd now to be satisfy'd, and make the best of their Way to the Island of Juan Fernando; where keeping at a great Distance from the Shore, they safely arriv'd, in about two Months Voyage, having met with some contrary Winds by the Way.

However, here they found the other Sloop which they had sent in with their first Booty, to wait for them: And here understanding that we were gone for St. Julien, they resolv'd, (since the Time was so long gone that they could not expect to find us again) that they would have t'other Touch with the Spaniards, cost what it would. And accordingly, having first bury'd the most Part of their Money in the Ground, on Shore in the Island, and having revictual'd their Ship in the best Manner they could in that barren Island, away they went to Sea.

They beat about on the South of the Line all up the Coast of Chili, and Part of Peru, till they came to the Height of Lima itself.

They met with several Ships, and took several, but they were loaden chiefly with Lumber or Provisions, except that in one Vessel they took between 40 and 50000 Pieces of Eight, and in another 75000. They soon inform'd themselves that the Spanish Men of War were gone out of those Seas up to Panama, to boast of their good Fortune, and carry Home their Prize; and this made them the bolder. But tho' they spent near five Months in this second Cruise, they met with nothing considerable; the Spaniards being every where alarm'd, and having Notice of them, so that nothing stirr'd Abroad.

Tir'd then with their long Cruise, and out of Hope of more Booty, they began to look Homeward, and to say to one another that they had enough; so, in a Word, they came back to Juan Fernando, and there furnishing themselves as well as they could with Provisions, and not forgeting to take their Treasure on Board with them, they set forward again to the South; and after a very bad Voyage in rounding the Terra del Fuego, being driven to the Latitude of 65 Degrees, where they felt Extremity of Cold, they at length obtain'd a more favourable Wind, viz. at S. and S. S. E; with which, steering to the North, they came into a milder Sea and a milder Coast, and at length arriv'd at Port St. Julien, where, to their great Joy, they found the Post or Cross erected by us; and understanding that we were gone to Madagascar, and that we would be sure to remain there to hear from them, and withal that we had been gone there near two Year, they resolv'd to follow us.

Here they staid, it seems, almost half a Year, partly fitting and altering their Ship, partly wearing out the Winter Season, and waiting for milder Weather; and having victuall'd their Ship in but a very ordinary Manner for so long a Run, viz. only with Seals Flesh and Penguins, and some Deer they kill'd in the Country, they at last launch'd out, and crossing the great Atlantick Ocean, they made the Cape of Good Hope in about 76 Days, having been put to very great Distresses in that Time for Want of Food, all their Seals Flesh and Penguins growing nauseous and stinking in little less than half the Time of their Voyage; so that they had nothing to subsist on for seven and twenty Days, but a little Quantity of dry'd Venison which they kill'd on Shore, about the Quantity of 3 Barrels of English Beef, and some Bread; and when they came to the Cape of Good Hope, they gat some small Supply, but it being soon perceiv'd on Shore what they were, they were glad to be gone as soon as they had fill'd their Casks with Water, and gat but a very little Provisions; so they made to the Coast of Natal on the South East Point of Africa, and there they gat more fresh Provisions, such as Veal, Milk, Goats-Flesh, some tolerable Butter, and very good Beef: And this held them out till they found us in the North Part of Madagascar, as above.

We staid about a Fortnight in our Port, and in a sailing Posture, just as if we had been Wind-bound, meerly to congratulate and make merry with our new-come Friends, when I resolv'd to leave them there, and set Sail; which I did with a Westerly Wind, keeping away North till I came into the Latitude of seven Degrees North; so coasting along the Arabian Coast E. N. E. towards the Gulph of Persia, in the Cruise I met with two Persian Barks loaden with Rice; one of which I mann'd and sent away to Madagascar, and the other I took for our own Ship's Use. This Bark came safe to my new Colony, and was a very agreeable Prize to them; I think verily almost as agreeable as if it had been loaded with Pieces of Eight, for they had been without Bread a great while; and this was a double Benefit to them, for they fitted up this Bark, which carry'd about 55 Tun, and went away to the Gulph of Persia in her to buy Rice, and brought two or three Freights of that which was very good.

In this Time I pursu'd my Voyage, coasted the whole Malabar Shore, and met with no Purchase but a great Portugal East-India Ship, which I chac'd into Goa, where she got out of my Reach: I took several small Vessels and Barks, but little of Value in them, till I enter'd the great Bay of Bengale, when I began to look about me with more Expectation of Success, tho' without Prospect of what happen'd.

I cruis'd here about two Months, finding nothing worth while; so I stood away to a Port on the North Point of the Isle of Sumatra, where I made no Stay; for here I gat News that two large Ships, belonging to the Great Mogul, were expected to cross the Bay from Hugely in the Ganges to the Country of the King of Pegu, being to carry the Grandaughter of the Great Mogul to Pegu, who was to be marry'd to the King of that Country, with all her Retinue, Jewels, and Wealth.

This was a Booty worth watching for, tho' it had been some Months longer; so I refolv'd that we would go and Cruise off of Point Negaris, on the East Side of the Bay, near Diamond Isle; and here we ply'd off and on for three Weeks, and began to despair of Success; but the Knowledge of the Booty we expected spurr'd us on, and we waited with great Patience, for we knew the Prize would be immensely rich.

At length we spy'd three Ships coming right up to us with the Wind; we could easily see they were not Europeans by their Sails, and began to prepare ourselves for a Prize, not for a Fight; but were a little disappointed, when we found the first Ship full of Guns, and full of Soldiers, and in Condition, had she been manag'd by English Sailors, to have fought two such Ships as ours were; however, we resolv'd to attack her if she had been full of Devils as she was full of Men.

Accordingly, when we came near them, we fir'd a Gun with Shot as a Challenge; they fir'd again immediately three or four Guns; but fir'd them so confusedly that we could easily see they did not understand their Business; when we consider'd how to lay them on Board, and so to come thwart them, if we could; but falling, for want of Wind, open to them, we gave them a fair Broadside; we could easily see, by the Confusion that was on Board, that they were frighted out of their Wits; they fir'd here a Gun and there a Gun, and some on that Side that was from us, as well as those that were next to us. The next Thing we did was to lay them on Board, which we did presently, and then gave them a Volley of our Small-shot, which, as they stood so thick, kill'd a great many of them, and made all the rest run down under their Hatches, crying out like Creatures bewitch'd: In a Word, we presently took the Ship, and having secur'd her Men, we chac'd the other two: One was chiefly fill'd with Women, and the other with Lumber. Upon the Whole, as the Grandaughter of the Great Mogul was our Prize in the first Ship, so, in the second was her Women, or, in a Word, her Houshold, her Eunuchs, all the Necessaries of her Wardrobe, of her Stables, and of her Kitchin; and in the last, great Quantities of Houshold-stuff, and Things less costly, tho' not less useful.

But the first was the main Prize. When my Men had enter'd and master'd the Ship, one of our Lieutenants call'd for me, and accordingly I jump'd on Board; he told me, he thought no Body but I ought to go into the great Cabin, or, at least, no Body should go there before me; for that the Lady herself and all her Attendance was there, and he fear'd the Men were so heated they would murder them all, or do worse.

I immediately went to the great Cabin-door, taking the Lieutenant that call'd me, along with me, and caus'd the Cabin-door to be open'd: But such a Sight of Glory and Misery was never seen by Buccaneer before; the Queen (for such she was to have been) was all in Gold and Silver, but frighted; and crying, and at the Sight of me she appear'd trembling, and just as if she was going to die. She sate on the Side of a kind of a Bed like a Couch with no Canopy over it, or any Covering, only made to lie down upon; she was, in a Manner, cover'd with Diamonds, and I, like a true Pirate, soon let her see that I had more Mind to the Jewels than to the Lady.

However, before I touch'd her, I order'd the Lieutenant to place a Guard at the Cabin-door; and fastening the Door, shut us both in, which he did: The Lady was young, and, I suppose, in their Country Esteem, very handsome, but she was not very much so in my Thoughts: At first, her Fright, and the Danger she thought she was in of being kill'd, taught her to do every Thing that she thought might interpose between her and Danger; and that was to take off her Jewels as fast as she could, and give them to me; and I, without any great Compliment, took them as fast as she gave them me, and put them into my Pocket, taking no great Notice of them, or of her, which frighted her worse than all the rest, and she said something which I could not understand; however, two of the other Ladies came, all crying, and kneel'd down to me with their Hands lifted up: What they meant I knew not at first, but by their Gestures and Pointings I found at last it was to beg the young Queen's Life, and that I would not kill her.

I have heard that it has been reported in England that I ravish'd this Lady, and then used her most barbarously; but they wrong me, for I never offer'd any Thing of that Kind to her, I assure you; nay, I was so far from being inclin'd to it, that I did not like her; and there was one of her Ladies who I found much more agreeable to me, and who I was afterwards something free with, but not even with her either by Force, or by Way of Ravishing.

We did, indeed, ravish them of all their Wealth, for that was what we wanted, not the Women; nor was there any other Ravishing among those in the great Cabin, that I can assure you: As for the Ship where the Women of inferior Rank were, and who were in Number almost two hundred, I cannot answer for what might happen in the first Heat; but even there, after the first Heat of our Men was over, what was done, was done quietly, for I have heard some of the Men say, that there was not a Woman among them but what was lain with four or five Times over, that is to say, by so many several Men; for as the Women made no Opposition, so the Men even took those that were next them, without Ceremony, when and where Opportunity offer'd.

When the three Ladies kneel'd down to me, and as soon as I understood what it was for, I let them know I would not hurt the Queen, nor let any one else hurt her, but that she must give me all her Jewels and Money: Upon this they acquainted her that I would save her Life; and no sooner had they assur'd her of that, but she got up, smiling, and went to a fine Indian Cabinet, and open'd a private Drawer, from whence she took another little Thing full of little square Drawers and Holes; this she brings to me in her Hand, and offer'd to kneel down to give it me. This innocent Usage began to rouse some Good-Nature in me, (tho' I never had much) and I would not let her kneel; but sitting down myself on the Side of her Couch or Bed, made a Motion to her to sit down too: But here she was frighted again, it seems, at what I had no Thought of; for sitting on her Bed, she thought I would pull her down to lie with her, and so did all her Women too; for they began to hold their Hands before their Faces, which, as I understood afterwards, was that they might not see me turn up their Queen: But as I did not offer any Thing of that

Kind, only made her sit down by me, they began all to be easier after some Time, and she gave me the little Box or Casket, I know not what to call it, but it was full of invaluable Jewels. I have them still in my Keeping, and wish they were safe in England; for I doubt not but some of them are fit to be plac'd on the King's Crown.

Being Master of this Treasure, I was very willing to be good-humour'd to the Persons; so I went out of the Cabin, and caus'd the Women to be left alone, causing the Guard to be kept still, that they might receive no more Injury than I would do them myself.

After I had been out of the Cabin some Time, a Slave of the Womens came to me, and made Sign to me that the Queen would speak with me again. I made Signs back, that I would come and dine with her Majesty: And accordingly I order'd that her Servants should prepare her Dinner, and carry it in, and then call me. They provided her Repast after the usual Manner, and when she saw it brought in, she appear'd pleas'd, and more, when she saw me come in after it; for she was exceedingly pleas'd that I had caus'd a Guard to keep the rest of my Men from her; and she had, it seems, been told how rude they had been to some of the Women that belong'd to her.

When I came in, she rose up, and paid me such Respect as I did not well know how to receive, and not in the least how to return. If she had understood English, I could have said plainly, and in good rough Words, Madam, be easy, we are rude rough-hewn Fellows, but none of our Men should hurt you, or touch you; I will be your Guard and Protection; we are for Money, indeed and we shall take what you have, but we will do you no other Harm. But as I could not talk thus to her, I scarce knew what to say; but I sate down, and made Signs to have her sit down and eat, which she did, but with so much Ceremony, that I did not know well what to do with it.

After we had eaten, she rose up again, and drinking some Water out of a China Cup, sate her down on the Side of the Couch, as before: When she saw I had done eating, she went then to another Cabinet, and pulling out a Drawer, she brought it to me; it was full of small Pieces of Gold Coin of Pegu, about as big as an English Half Guinea, and I think there were three thousand of them. She open'd several other Drawers, and shew'd me the Wealth that was in them and then gave me the Key of the Whole.

We had revell'd thus all Day, and Part of the next Day, in a bottomless Sea of Riches, when my Lieutenant began to tell me, we must consider what to do with our Prisoners, and the Ships, for that there was no subsisting in that Manner; besides, he hinted privately, that the Men would be ruin'd, by lying with the Women in the other Ship, where all Sorts of Liberty was both given and taken: Upon this we call'd a short Council, and concluded to carry the great Ship away with us, but to put all the Prisoners, Queen, Ladies, and all the rest, into the lesser Vessels, and let them go: And so far was I from ravishing this Lady, as I hear is reported of me, that tho' I might rifle her of every Thing else, yet I assure you I let her go untouch'd for me, or, as I am satisfy'd, for any one, of my Men; nay, when we dismiss'd them, we gave her Leave to take a great many Things of Value with her, which she would have been plunder'd of, if I had not been so careful of her.

We had now Wealth enough, not only to make us rich, but almost to have made a Nation rich; and to tell you the Truth, considering the costly Things we took here, which we did not know the Value of, and besides Gold, and Silver, and Jewels, I say, we never knew how rich we were; besides which, we had a great Quantity of Bales of Goods, as well Calicoes as wrought Silks; which being for Sale, were, perhaps, as a Cargo of Goods to answer the Bills which might be drawn upon them for the Account of the Bride's

Portion; all which fell into our Hands, with a great Sum in Silver Coin, too big to talk of among Englishmen, especially while I am living, for Reasons which I may give you hereafter.

I had nothing to do now but to think of coming back to Madagascar, so we made the best of our Way; only that, to make us quite distracted without other Joy, we took in our Way a small Bark loaden with Arack and Rice, which was good Sawce to our other Purchace; for if the Women made our Men drunk before, this Arack made them quite mad; and they had so little Government of themselves with it, that I think it might be said, the whole Ship's Crew was drunk for above a Fortnight together, till six or seven of them kill'd themselves; two fell overboard and were drown'd, and several more fell into raging Fevers, and it was a Wonder, in the whole, they were not all kill'd with it.

But, to make short of the Story as we did of the Voyage, we had a very pleasant Voyage, except those Disasters, and we came safe back to our Comrades at Madagascar, having been absent in all about seven Months.

We found them in very good Health, and longing to hear from us; and we were, you may be assur'd, welcome to them; for now we had amass'd such a Treasure as no Society of Men ever possess'd in this World before us, neither could we ever bring it to an Estimation, for we could not bring particular Things to a just Valuation.

We liv'd now and enjoy'd ourselves in full Security; for tho' some of the European Nations, and perhaps all of them had heard of us; yet they heard such formidable Things of us, such terrible Stories of our great Strength, as well as of our great Wealth, that they had no Thought of undertaking any Thing against us; for, as I have understood, they were told at London, that we were no less than 5000 Men; that we had built a regular Fortress for our Defence by Land, and that we had 20 Sail of Ships; and I have been told that in France they have heard the same Thing: But nothing of all this was ever true, any more than it was true, that we offer'd ten Millions to the Government of England for our Pardon.

It is true, that had the Queen sent any Intimation to us of a Pardon, and that we should have been receiv'd to Grace at Home, we should all have very willingly embrac'd it; for we had Money enough to have encourag'd us all to live honest; and if we had been ask'd for a Million of Pieces of Eight, or a Million of Pounds Sterling, to have purchas'd our Pardon, we should have been very ready to have comply'd with it; for we really knew not what to do with ourselves, or with our Wealth; and the only Thing we had now before us, was to consider what Method to take for getting Home, if possible, to our own Country with our Wealth, or at least with such Part of it as would secure us easy and comfortable Lives; and, for my own Part, I resolv'd, if I could, to make full Satisfaction to all the Persons who I had wrong'd in England, I mean by that, such People as I had injur'd by running away with the Ship; as well the Owners, and the Master or Captain, who I set a-shore in Spain, as the Merchant whose Goods I had taken with the Ship; and I was daily forming Schemes in my Thoughts how to bring this to pass: But we all concluded that it was impossible for us to accomplish our Desires as to that Part, seeing the Fact of our Piracy was now so publick all over the World, that there was not any Nation in the World that would receive us, or any of us; but would immediately seize on our Wealth, and execute us for Pirates and Robbers of all Nations.

This was confirm'd to us after some Time, with all the Particulars, as it is now understood in Europe; for as the Fame of our Wealth and Power was such, that it made all the World afraid of us, so it brought some of the like Sort with our selves to join with us from all Parts of the World; and particularly, we had a Bark, and 60 Men of all Nations, from Martinico, who had been cruising in the Gulph of Florida, came over to us, to try if they could mend their Fortunes; and these went afterwards to the Gulph of Persia, where they took some Prizes, and return'd to us again. We had after this three Pirate Ships came to us, most English, who had done some Exploits on the Coast of Guinea, had made several good Prizes, and were all tolerably rich.

As these People came and shelter'd with us, so they came and went as they would, and sometimes some of our Men went with them, sometimes theirs staid with us: But by that Coming and Going our Men found Ways and Means to convey themselves away, some one Way, some another. For I should have told you at first, that after we had such Intelligence from England, viz. that they knew of all our successful Enterprizes, and that there was no Hopes of our returning, especially of mine and some other Men who were known: I say, after this we call'd a general Council to consider what to do; and there, one and all, we concluded that we liv'd very happy where we were; that if any of us had a Mind to venture to get away to any Part of the World, none should hinder them, but that else we would continue where we were; and that the first Opportunity we had we would cruise upon the English East India Ships, and do them what Spoil we could, fancying that some Time or other they would proclaim a Pardon to us, if we would come in; and if they did, then we would accept of it.

Under these Circumstances we remain'd here, off and on, first and last, above three Year more; during which Time our Number encreas'd so, especially at first, that we were once eight hundred Men, stout brave Fellows, and as good Sailors as any in the World. Our Number decreas'd afterwards upon several Occasions; such as the going Abroad to Cruise, wandering to the South Part of the Island, (as above) getting on Board European Ships, and the like.

After I perceiv'd that a great many of our Men were gone off, and had carry'd their Wealth with them, I began to cast about in my own Thoughts how I should make my Way Home also: Innumerable Difficulties presented to my View; when at last, an Account of some of our Mens Escape into Persia encourag'd me. The Story was this: One of the small Barks we had taken, went to Guzaratte to get Rice, and having secur'd a Cargo, but not loaded it, ten of our Men resolv'd to attempt their Escape; and accordingly they drest themselves like Merchant-Strangers, and bought several Sorts of Goods there, such as an Englishman, who they found there, assisted them to buy; and with their Bales, (but in them pack'd up all the rest of their Money) they went up to Bassora in the Gulph of Persia, and so travell'd as Merchants with the Caravan to Aleppo, and we never heard any more of them, but that they went clean off with all their Cargo.

This fill'd my Head with Schemes for my own Deliverance; but however, it was a Year more before I attempted any Thing, and not till I found that many of our Men shifted off, some and some, nor did any of them miscarry; some went one Way, some another; some lost their Money, and some sav'd it; nay, some carry'd it away with them, and some left it behind them: As for me, I discover'd my Intentions to no Body, but made them all believe I would stay here till some of them should come and fetch me off, and pretended to make every Man that went off promise to come for me, if it ever was in his Power, and gave every one of them Signals to make for me, when they came back, upon which I would certainly come off to them. At the same Time nothing was more certain, than that I intended from the Beginning to get away from the Island, as soon as I could any Way make my Way with Safety to any Part of the World.

It was still above two Years after this that I remain'd in the Island; nor could I, in all that Time, find any probable Means for removing my self with Safety.

One of the Ways I thought to have made my Escape was this: I went to Sea in a Long-boat a fishing, (as we often did) and having a Sail to the Boat, we were out two or three Days together; at length it came into my Thoughts that we might Cruise about the Island in this Long-boat, a great Way, and perhaps some Adventure might happen to us which we might make something of; so I told them I had a Mind to make a Voyage with the Long-boat to see what would happen.

To this Purpose we built upon her, made a State-Room in the Middle, and clapt four Patareroes upon her Gunnel, and away we went, being sixteen stout Fellows in the Boat, not reckoning my self: Thus we ran away, as it were, from the rest of our Crew, tho' not a Man of us knew our own Minds as to whither we were going, or upon what Design. In this Frolick we ran South quite away to the Bay of St. Angustine's, in the Latitude of 24 Degrees, where the Ships from Europe often put in for Water and Provisions.

Here we put in, not knowing well what to do next; I thought myself disappointed very much that we saw no European Ship here, tho' afterwards I saw my Mistake, and found that it was better for us that we were in that Port first: We went boldly on Shore; for as to the Natives, we understood how to manage them well enough, knew all their Customs, and the Manner of their treating with Strangers as to Peace or War; their Temper, and how to oblige them, or behave if they were disoblig'd; so we went, I say, boldly on Shore, and there we began to chaffer with them for some Provisions, such as we wanted.

We had not been here above two or three Days, but that, early in the Morning, the Weather thick and haizy, we heard several Guns fire at Sea; we were not at a Loss to know what they meant, and that it was certainly some European Ships coming in, and who gave the Signal to one another that they had made the Land, which they could easily see from the Sea, tho' we, who were also within the Bay, could not see them from the Shore: However, in a few Hours, the Weather clearing up, wet saw plainly five large Ships, three with English Colours, and two with Dutch, standing into the Bay, and in about four or five Hours more they came to an Anchor.

A little while after they were come to an Anchor, their Boats began to come on Shore to the usual Watering-place to fill their Casks; and while they were doing that, the rest of the Men look'd about them a little, as usual, tho' at first they did not stir very far from their Boats.

I had now a nice Game to play, as any Man in the World ever had: It was absolutely necessary for us to speak with these Men; and yet how to speak with them, and not have them speak with us in a Manner that we should not like, that was the main Point: It was with a great deal of Impatience that we lay still one whole Day, and saw their Boats come on Shore, and go on Board again, and we were so irresolute all the while, that we knew not what to do; at last I told my Men, it was absolutely necessary we should speak with them, and seeing we could not agree upon the Method how to do it friendly and fairly, I was resolv'd to do it by Force, and that if they would take my Advice, we would place ourselves in Ambuscade upon the Land somewhere, that we might see them when they were on Shore, and the first Man that straggled from the rest we would clap in upon and seize him, and three or four of them if we could. As for our Boat, we had secur'd it in a Creek three or four Miles up the Country, where it was secure enough out of their Reach or Knowledge.

With this Resolution we plac'd ourselves in two Gangs; eleven of us in one Place, and only three of us in another, and very close we lay: The Place we chose for our Ambuscade was on the Side of a rising Ground almost a Mile from the Watering-place, but where we could see them all come towards the Shore, and see them if they did but set their Foot on Shore.

As we understood afterwards, they had the Knowledge of our being upon the Island, but knew not in what Part of it, and were therefore very cautious and wary how they went on Shore, and came all very well arm'd. This gave us a new Difficulty, for in the very first Excursion that any of them made from the Watering-place, there was not less than twenty of them, all well arm'd, and they pass'd by in our Sight; but as we were out of their Sight we were all very well pleas'd with seeing them go by, and being not oblig'd to meddle with them, or show our selves.

But we had not long lain in this Circumstance, but, by what Occasion we knew not, five of the Gentlemen Tarrs were pleas'd to be willing to go no farther with their Companions; and thinking all safe behind them, because they had found no Disturbance in their going out, came back the same Way, straggling without any Guard or Regard.

I thought now was our Time to show our selves; so taking them as they came by the Place where we lay in Ambuscade, we plac'd ourselves just in their Way, and as they were entring a little Thicket of Trees, we appear'd; and calling to them in English, told them they were our Prisoners; that if they yielded, we would use them very well, but if they offer'd to resist, they should have no Quarter: One of them looking behind, as if he would show us a Pair of Heels, I call'd to him, and told him, if he attempted to run for it, he was a dead Man, unless he could out-run a Musquet-Bullet; and that we would soon let him see we had more Men in our Company; and so giving the Signal appointed, our three Men, who lay at a Distance, shew'd themselves in the Rear.

When they saw this, one of them, who appear'd as their Leader, but was only the Purser's Clerk, ask'd, Who we were they must yield to? And if we were Christians? I told them, jestingly, We were good honest Christian Pirates, and belong'd to Captain Avery, (not at all letting them know that I was Avery himself) and if they yielded it was enough; that we assur'd them they should have fair Quarter and good Usage upon our Honour; but that they must resolve immediately, or else they would be surrounded with 500 Men, and we could not answer for what they might do to them.

They yielded presently upon this News, and deliver'd their Arms; and we carry'd them away to our Tent, which we had built near the Place where our Boat lay. Here I enter'd into a particular serious Discourse with them about Captain Avery, for 'twas this I wanted, upon several Accounts: First, I wanted to enquire what News they had had of us in Europe? and then to give them Ideas of our Numbers and Power as romantick as I could.

They told us, that they had heard of the great Booty Captain Avery had taken in the Bay of Bengale; and among the rest, a bloody Story was related of Avery himself, viz. That he ravish'd the Great Mogul's Daughter, who was going to be marry'd to the Prince of Pegu; that we ravish'd and forc'd all the Ladies attending her Train, and then threw them into the Sea, or cut their Throats; and that we had gotten a Booty of ten Millions in Gold and Silver, besides an inestimable Treasure of Jewels, Diamonds, Pearls, &c. but that we had committed most inhuman Barbarities on the innocent People that fell into our Hands. They then told us, but in a broken imperfect Account, how the Great Mogul had resented it; and that he had raised a great Army against the English Factories, resolving to root them out of his Dominions; but that the Company had appeas'd him by Presents, and by assuring him that the Men who did it, were Rebels to the English Government, and that the Queen of England would hang them all when ever they could be taken. I smil'd at that, and told them, Captain Avery would give them Leave to hang him, and all his Men, when they could take them; but that I could assure him they were too strong to be taken; that if the Government of England went about to provoke them, Captain Avery would soon make those Seas too hot for the English, and they might even give over their East-India Trade, for they little thought Circumstances Captain Avery was in.

This I did, as well to know what Notions you had of us in England, as to give a formidable Account of us, and of our Circumstances to England, which I knew might be of Use to us several Ways hereafter. Then I made him tell his Part, which he did freely enough; he told us, that indeed they had receiv'd an Account in England that we were exceeding strong; that we had several Gangs of Pirates from the Spanish West-Indies, that had taken great Booties there, and were gone all to Madagascar to join Captain Avery; that he had taken three great East-India Ships, one Dutch, and two Portuguese, which they had converted into Men of War; that he had 6000 Men under his Command; that he had twelve Ships, whereof three carry'd 60 Guns a-piece, and six more of them, from 40 to 50 Guns; that they had built a large Fort to secure their Habitations; and that they had two large Towns, one on one Side, one on the other of a River, cover'd by the said Fort, and two great Platforms or Batteries of Guns to defend the Entrance where their Ships rode; that they had an immense invaluable Treasure; and that it was said, Captain Avery was resolv'd to People the whole Island of Madagascar with Europeans, and to get Women from Jamaica and the Leeward Islands; and that it was not doubted but he would subdue, and make himself King of that Country, if he was let alone a little longer.

I had enjoin'd my Men, in the first Place, not to let him know that I was Avery, but that I was one of his Captains; and in the next Place, not to say a Word but just Ay, and No, as Things occurr'd, and leave the rest to me. I heard him patiently out in all the Particulars above, and when he had done, I told him it was true, Captain Avery was in the Island of Madagascar, and that several other Societies of Buccaneers and Freebooters were join'd him from the Spanish West-Indies; for, said I, the Plenty and Ease of our living here is such, and we are so safe from all the World, that we do not doubt but we shall be twenty thousand Men in a very little Time, when two Ships which we have sent to the West-Indies shall come back, and shall have told the Buccaneers at the Bay of Campeachy, how we live here.

But, said I, you in England greatly wrong Captain Avery, our General, (so I call'd myself, to advance our Credit) for I can assure you, that except plundering the Ship, and taking that immense Booty which he got in the great Ship where the Great Mogul's Daughter was, there was not the least Injury done to the Lady, no Ravishing or Violence to her, or any of her Attendance; and this, said I, you may take of my certain Knowledge; for, said I, I was on Board the Ship with our General all the while: And if any of the Princess's Women were lain with, said I, on Board the other Ship, as I believe most of them were, yet it was done with their own Consent and good Will, and no otherwise; and they were all dismiss'd afterwards, without so much as being put in Fear or Apprehensions of Life or Honour.

This I assur'd him, (as indeed it was just) and told him, I hop'd, if ever he came safe to England, he would do Captain Avery, and all of us, Justice in that particular Case.

As to our being well fortify'd on the Island, and our Numbers, I assur'd them all they were far from thinking too much of us; that we had a very good Fleet, and a very good Harbour for them; that we were not afraid of any Force from Europe, either by Land or Water; that it was, indeed, in vain to pretend to attack us by Force; that the only Way for the Government of England to bring us back to our Duty, would be to send a Proclamation from England with the Queen's Pardon for our General and all his People, if they came in by a certain Time: And, added I, we know you want Money in England, I dare say, said I, our General, Captain Avery, and his particular Gang, who have the main Riches, would not grudge to advance five or six Millions of Ducats to the Government, to give them Leave to return in Peace to England, and sit down quietly with the rest.

This Discourse, I suppose, was the Ground of the Rumour you have had in England, That Avery had offer'd to come in and submit, and would give six Millions for his Pardon: For as these Men were soon after this dismiss'd, and went back to England, there is no Doubt but they gave a particular Account of the Conference they had with me, who they call'd one of Captain Avery's Captains.

We kept these five Men six or seven Days, and we pretended to show them the Country from some of the Hills, calling it all our own, and pointing every Way how many Miles we extended ourselves; we made them believe also that all the rest of the Country was at our Disposal, that the whole Island was at our Beck; we told them we had Treasure enough to enrich the whole Kingdom of England; that our General had several Millions in Diamonds, and we had many Tuns of Silver and Gold; that we had fifty large Barns full of all Sorts of Goods, as well European as Indian; and that it would be truly the best Way for England to do as they said, namely, to invite us all Home by a Proclamation with a Pardon: And if they would do this, said I, they can ask no reasonable Sum, but our General might advance it; besides, getting Home such a Body of stout able Seamen as we were, such a Number of Ships, and such a Quantity of rich Goods.

We had several long Discourses with them upon these Heads, and our frequent offering this Part to them with a Kind of feeling Warmth, (for it was what we all desir'd) has caus'd, I doubt not, the Rumour of such great Offers made by us, and of a Letter sent by me to the Queen, to beg her Majesty's Pardon for myself and my Company, and offering ten Millions of Money Advance to the Queen for the publick Service: All which is a meer Fiction of the Brain of those which have publish'd it; neither were we in any Condition to make such an Offer; neither did I, or any of my Crew or Company, ever write a Letter or Petition to the Queen, or to any one in the Government, or make any Application in the Case other than as above, which was only Matter of Conversation or private Discourse.

Nor were we so strong in Men or Ships, or any Thing like it. You have heard of the Number of Ships which we had now with us, which amounted to two Ships and a Sloop, and no more, except the Prize in which we took the Mogul's Daughter; (which Ship we call'd, The Great Mogul) but she was fit for nothing, for she would neither sail or steer worth a Farthing, and indeed was fit for no Use but a Hulk, or a Guard-Ship.

As to Numbers of Men, they bely'd us strangely, and particularly, they seem'd only to mistake Thousands for Hundreds: For whereas they told us, that you in England had a Report of our being six thousand Men, I must acknowledge that I think we were never, when we were at the most, above six hundred; and at the Time when I quitted the Country, I left about one hundered and eight Men there, and no more, and I am assur'd, all the Number that now remains there, is not above twenty two Men, no, not in the whole Island.

Well, we thought, however, that it was no Business of ours at that Time to undeceive them in their high Opinion of our great Strength, so we took Care to magnify ourselves, and the Strength of our General, (meaning myself) that they might carry the Story to England, depending upon it, That a Tale loses nothing in the carrying. When they told us of our Fort, and the Batteries at the Mouth of the River where our Ships lie, we insinuated, that it was a Place where we did not fear all the Fleets in the World attacking us; and when they told us of the Number of Men, we strove to make them believe that they were much many more.

At length, the poor Men began to be tir'd of us, and indeed we began to be tir'd of them; for we began to be afraid very much that they would prye a little Way into our Affairs, and that a little too narrowly that Way; so as they began to sollicit their Deliverance, we began to listen to their Importunities: In a Word, we agreed to dismiss them; and accordingly we gave them Leave to go away to the Watering-place, as if they had made their Escape from us; which they did, carrying away their Heads full of all those unlikely projected Things which you have heard above.

In all this, however, I had not the good Luck to advance one Step towards my own Escape; and here is one Thing remarkable, viz. That the great Mass of Wealth I had gotten together, was so far from forwarding my Deliverance, that it really was the only Thing that hinder'd it most effectually; and I was so sensible of it, that I resolv'd once to be gone, and leave all my Wealth behind me, except some Jewels, as several of our Men had done already: For many of them were so impatient of staying here, that they found Means to get away, some and some, with no more Money than they could carry about them; particularly, thirteen of our Men made themselves a Kind of Shaloup with a Mast and Sail, and went for the Red Sea, having two Patareroes for her Defence, and every Man a thousand Pieces of Eight, and no more, except that one Macmow an Irishman, who was their Captain, had five Rubies and a Diamond, which he got among the Plunder of the Mogul's Ship.

These Men, as I heard, gat safe to Mocca in the Arabian Gulph, where they fetch the Coffee, and their Captain manag'd for them all so well, that of Pirates he made them Merchants, laid out all the Stock in Coffee, and got a Vessel to carry it up the Red Sea to Sues, where they sold it to the Factors for the European Merchants, and came all safe to Alexandria, where they parted the Money again; and then every one separated as they thought fit, and went their own Way.

We heard of this by mere Accident afterwards, and I confess I envy'd their Success; and tho' it was a great while after this that I took a like Run, yet you may be sure I form'd a Resolution from that Time to do the like; and most of the Time that I stay'd after this, was employ'd in picking out a suitable Gang that I might depend upon, as well to trust with the Secret of my going away, as to take with me; and on whom I might depend, and they on me, for keeping one another's Council when we should come into Europe.

It was in Pursuit of this Resolution that I went this little Voyage to the South of the Island, and the Gang I took with me prov'd very trusty, but we found no Opportunity then for our Escape: Two of the Men that we took Prisoners would fain have gone with us, but we resolv'd to trust none of them with the real and true Discovery of our Circumstances; and as we had made them believe mighty Things of ourselves, and of the Posture of our Settlement, that we had 5000 Men, 12 Men of War, and the like, we were resolv'd they should carry the Delusion away with them, and that no Body should undeceive them; because, tho' we had not such an immense Wealth as was reported, and so as to be able to offer ten Millions for our Pardon, yet we had a very great Treasure; and, being nothing near so strong as they had imagin'd, we might have been made a Prey, with all our Riches, to any Set of Adventurers who might undertake to attempt us, by Consent of the Government of England, and make the Expedition, No Purchase no Pay.

For this Reason we civily declin'd them, told them we had Wealth enough, and therefore did not now Cruise Abroad as we used to do, unless we should hear of another Wedding of a King's Daughter; or unless some rich Fleet, or some Heathen Kingdom was to be attempted; and that therefore a new Comer, or any Body of new Comers, could do themselves no good by coming over to us: If any Gang of Pirates or Buccaneers would go upon their Adventures, and when they had made themselves rich, would come and settle with us, we would take them into our Protection, and give them Land to build

Towns and Habitations for themselves, and so in Time we might become a great Nation, and inhabit the whole Island: I told them, the Romans themselves were, at first, no better than such a Gang of Rovers as we were; and who knew but our General, Captain Avery, might lay the Foundation of as great an Empire as they.

These big Words amaz'd the Fellows, and answer'd my End to a Tittle; for they told such Rhodomantading Stories of us, when they came back to their Ships, and from them it spread so universally all over the East-Indies, (for they were Outward-bound) that none of the English or Dutch Ships would come near Madagascar again, if they could help it, for a great while, for Fear of us; and we, who were soon after this dwindled away to less than 100 Men, were very glad to have them think us too strong to meddle with, or so strong that no Body durst come near us.

After these Men were gone, we rov'd about to the East Side of the Island, and in a Word, knew not what to do, or what Course to take, for we durst not put out to Sea in such a Bauble of a Boat as we had under us; but tir'd at last, we came back to the South Point of the Island again; in our rounding the Island we saw a great English-built Ship at Sea, but at too far Distance to speak with her; and if it had not, we knew not what to have said to her, for we were not strong enough to attack her: We judg'd by her Course, she stood away from the Isle of St. Maurice or Mauritius, for the Cape of Good Hope, and must, as we suppos'd, come from the Malabar Coast, bound Home for England; so we let her go.

We are now return'd back to our Settlement on the North Part of the Island; and I have singl'd out about 12 or 13 bold brave Fellows, with whom I am resolv'd to venture to the Gulph of Persia; twenty more of our Men have agreed to carry us thither as Passengers in the Sloop, and try their own Fortunes afterwards, for they allow we are enough to go together. We resolve, when we come to Bassaro, to separate into three Companies, as if we did not know one another; to dress ourselves as Merchants, for now we look like Hell-hounds and Vagabonds; but when we are well dress'd, we expect to look as other Men do. If I come thither, I purpose, with two more, to give my Companions the Slip, and travel as Armenians thro' Persia to the Caspian Sea, so to Constantinople; and I doubt not we shall, one Way or other, find our Way, with our Merchandize and Money, to come into France, if not quite Home to my own Country. Assure yourself, when I arrive in any Part of Christendom, I will give you a farther Account of my Adventures.

Your Friend and Servant,

AVERY.

The End of the First Letter.

A SECOND LETTER

SIR,

I wrote my last Letter to you from Madagascar, where I had continu'd so long till my People began to drop from me, some and some, and, indeed, I had, at last, but few left; so that I began to apprehend they would give an Account in Europe, how weak I was, and how easy it was to attack me; nay, and to make their Peace, might some of them, at least, offer their Service to be Pilots to my Port, and might guide the Fleets or Ships that should attempt me.

With these Apprehensions, I not only was uneasy myself, but made all my Men uneasy too; for, as I was resolv'd to attempt my own Escape, I did not care how many of my Men went before me: But this you must take with you by the Bye, that I never let them imagine that I intended to stir from the Spot myself; I mean, after my Return from the Ramble that I had taken round the Island, of which I have given you an Account; but, that I resolv'd to take up my Rest in Madagascar as long as I liv'd; indeed, before, I said otherwise, as I wrote you before, and made them all promise to fetch me away, but now I gave it out that I was resolv'd to live and die here; and therefore, a little before I resolv'd upon going, I set to Work to build me a new House, and to plant me a pretty Garden at a Distance from our Fort; only I had a select Company, to whom I communicated every Thing, and who resolv'd that, at last, we would go altogether, but that we would do it our own Way.

When I had finish'd my new House, (and a mighty Palace you would say it was, if you had been to see it) I remov'd to it, with eight of the Gang that were to be my Fellow adventurers; and to this Place we carry'd all our private Wealth, that is to say, Jewels and Gold; as to our Share of Silver, as it was too heavy to remove, and must be done in Publick, I was oblig'd to leave it behind; but we had a Stratagem for that too, and it was thus:

We had a Sloop, as you have heard, and she lay in our Harbour, 'tis true; but she lay ready to sail upon any Occasion; and the Men, who were of our Confederacy, who were not with me at my Country-house, were twelve in Number: These Men made a Proposal, that they would take the Sloop, and go away to the Coast of Malabar, or where else they could speed to their Mind, and buy a Fraight of Rice for the publick Account: In a free State as we were, every Body was free to go wherever they would, so that no Body oppos'd them; the only Dispute at any Time, was about taking the Vessel we had to go in: However, as these Men seem'd only to act upon the publick Account, and to go to buy Provisions, no Body offer'd to deny them the Sloop, so they prepar'd for their Voyage: Just as they were ready to go, one of them starts it to the rest, that it was very hazardous and difficult to run such a Length every now and then to get a little Rice, and if they would go, why should they not bring a good Quantity? This was soon resolv'd; so they agreed, they should take Money with them to buy a good Ship wherever they could find her, and then to buy a Loading of Rice to fill her up, and so come away with her.

When this was agreed, they resolv'd to take no Money out of the grand Stock, but to take such Mens Money as were gone, and had left their Money behind; and this being consented to, truly, my Friends took the Occasion, and took all their own Money, and mine, (being 64 little Chests of Pieces of Eight) and carry'd it on Board, as if it had been of Men that were Prick'd-run, and no Body took any Notice of it. These twelve Men had also now got twelve more with them, under Pretence of manning a Ship, if we should buy one, and in this Pickle away they put to Sea.

We had due Notice of every Thing that was done; and having a Signal given of the Time they resolv'd to go, we pack'd up all our Treasure, and began our March to the Place appointed, which from our Quarters was about forty Mile farther North.

Our Habitation, that is to say, my new House, was about sixteen Miles up the Country, so that the rest of our People could have no Notice of our March, neither did they miss us, at least, as I heard of, for we never heard any more of them; nor can I imagine what Condition or Circumstance they can be in at present, if they are still upon the Place, as, however, I believe some of them are.

We join'd our Comrades, with a great Deal of Ease, about three Days afterwards, for we march'd but softly, and they lay by for us: The Night before we went on Board, we made them a Signal by Fire, as we had appointed to let them know where we were, and that we were at Hand; so they sent their Boat and fetch'd us off, and we embark'd without any Notice taken by the Rest.

As we were now loose, and at Sea, our next Business was to resolve whither we should go; and I soon govern'd the Point, resolving for Bassaro in the Gulph of Persia, where I knew we might shift for ourselves: Accordingly, we steer'd away for the Arabian Coast, and had good Weather for some Time, even till we made the Land at a great Distance, when we steer'd Eastward along the Shore.

We saw several Ships, in our Way, bound to and from the Red Sea, as we suppos'd, and, at another Time, we would have been sure to have spoken with them: But, we had done Pirating; our Business now was, how to get off, and make our Way to some Retreat, where we might enjoy what we had got; so we took no Notice of any Thing by the Way; but, when we was thus sailing merrily along, the Weather began to change, the Evening grew black and cloudy, and threaten'd a Storm: We were in Sight or a little Island, (I know nothing of its Name) under which we might have anchor'd with Safety enough, but our People made light of it, and went on.

About an Hour after Sun-set the Wind began to rise, and blew hard at N. E. and at N. E. by N. and in two Hours Time encreas'd to such a Tempest, as in all my Rambles I never met with the like; we were not able to carry a Knot of Sail, or to know what to do, but to stow every Thing close, and let her drive; and, in this Condition we continu'd all the Night, all the next Day, and Part of the Night after; towards Morning the Storm abated a little, but not so as to give us any Prospect of pursuing our voyage; all the Ease we had, was, that we could just carry a little Sail to steddy the Vessel, and run away before it; which we did at that violent Rate, that we never abated 'till we made Land on the East Side of Madagascar, the very Island we came from, only on the other Side of the Island.

However, we were glad we had any Place to run to for Harbour; so we put in under the Lee of a Point of Land that gave us Shelter from the Wind, and where we came to an Anchor, after being all of us almost dead with the Fatigue; and, if our Sloop had not been an extraordinary Sea-boat, she could never have born such a Sea, for twelve Days together, as we were in, the worst I ever saw before or since. We lay here, to refresh ourselves, about twenty Days; and, indeed, the Wind blew so hard all the while, that if we had been dispos'd to go to Sea, we could not have done it; and, being here, about seven of our Men began to repent their Bargain, and left us, which I was not sorry for. It seems, the principal Reason of their looking back, was, their being of those who had left their Money behind them. They did not leave us without our Consent, and therefore our Carpenters built them a Boat, during the three Weeks we stay'd here, and fitted it very handsomely for them, with a Cabin for their Convenience, and a Mast and Sail, with which they might very well sail round to our Settlement, as we suppose they did: We gave them Fire-arms and Ammunition sufficient, and left them furnishing themselves with Provisions; and this, we suppose, was the Boat, tho' with other Men in it, which adventur'd afterwards as far as the Cape of Good Hope, and was taken up by a Portugese in Distress, by which Means they got Passage for themselves to Lisbone, pretending they had made their Escape from the Pirates at Madagascar; but we were told, that the Portuguese Captain took a good deal of their Money from them, under Pretence of keeping it from his own Seamen; and that when they came on Shore, and began to claim it, he threaten'd them with taking them up, and prosecuting them for Pirates, which made them compound with him, and take about 10000 Dollars for above 120000, which they had with them; which, by the Way, was but a scurvy Trick: They had, it seems, a considerable Quantity of Gold among them, which they had the Wit to conceal from the Captain of the Ship, and which was enough for such Fellows as them, and more than they well knew what to do with; so that they were rich enough still, tho' the Portugal Captain was nevertheless a Knave for all that.

We left them here, as I have said, and put to Sea again; and, in about twenty Days Sail, having pretty good Weather, we arriv'd at the Gulph of Persia: It would be too long to give you an Account of the particular Fortunes of some of our People after this, the Variety of which would fill a Volume by itself: But, in the first Place, we, who were determin'd to travel, went on Shore at Bassaro, leaving the rest of our Men to buy Rice, and load the larger Vessel back to their Comrades, which they promis'd to do; but how far they perform'd I know not.

We were thirteen of us that went on Shore here; from whence we hir'd a kind of Barge, or rather a Bark, which, after much Difficulty, and very unhandy Doings of the Men who we had hir'd, brought us to Babylon, or Bagdat, as it is now call'd.

Our Treasure was so great, that if it had been known what we had about us, I am of Opinion we should never have troubl'd Europe with our Company: However, we gat safe to Babylon or Bagdat, where we kept ourselves Incog for a while, took a House by ourselves, and lay four or five Days still, till we had got Vests and long Gowns made to appear Abroad in as Armenian Merchants. After we had got Cloaths, and look'd like other People, we began to appear Abroad; and I, that from the Beginning had meditated my Escape by myself, began now to put it into Practice; and, walking one Morning upon the Bank of the River Euphrates, I mus'd with myself what Course I should take to make off, and get quite away from the Gang, and let them not so much as suspect me.

While I was walking here, comes up one of my Comrades, and one who I always took for my particular Friend: I know what you are employ'd in, said he, while you seem only to be musing, and refreshing yourself with the cool Breeze. Why, said I, what am I musing about? Why, said he, you are studying how you should get away from us; but, muse upon it as long as you will, says he, you shall never go without me, for I am resolv'd to go with you which Way soever you take. 'Tis true, says I, I was musing which Way I should go, but not which Way I should go without you; for tho' I would be willing to part Company, yet you cannot think I would go alone; and you know I have chosen you out from all the Company to be the Partner of all my Adventures.

Very well, says he, but I am to tell you now, that it is not only necessary that we should not go all together; but, our Men have all concluded, that we should make our Escape every one for himself, and should separate as we could; so that you need make no Secret of your Design any more than of the Way you intend to take.

I was glad enough of this News, and it made me very easy in the Preparations we made for our setting out: And, the first Thing we did, was, to get us more Cloaths, having some made of one Fashion, some of another; but, my Friend and I, who resolv'd to keep together, made us Cloaths after the Fashion of the Armenian Merchants, whose Country we pretended to travel through.

In the mean Time, five of our Men dress'd like Merchants; and, laying out their Money in Raw Silk, and Wrought Silks, and other Goods of the Country, proper for Europe, (in which they were directed by an English Merchant there) resolv'd to take the usual Rout, and travel by the Caravans from Babylon to Alleppo, and so to Scanderoon, and we staid and saw them and their Bales go off in Boats for a great Town on the Euphrates, where the Caravans begin to take up the Passengers; the other six divided themselves, one Half of them went for Agra, the Country of the Great Mogul, resolving to go down the River Hoogly to Bengal; but whither they went afterward or what Course they took, I never knew, neither whether they really went at all or not.

The other three went by Sea, in a Persian Vessel, back from the Red Sea to the Gulf of Mocca, and I heard of them all three at Marseilles; but whither they went afterwards I never knew, nor could I come to speak with them even there.

As for me and my Friend, we first laid out all the Silver we had in European Ware, such as we knew would vend at Ispahan, which we carry'd upon twelve Camels; and hiring some Servants, as well for our Guide as our Guard, we set out.

The Servants we hir'd were a Kind of Arab, but rather looking like the Great Mogul's people, than real Arabians; and when we came into Persia, we found they were look'd upon as no better than Dogs, and were not only used ill, but that we were used ill for their Sakes; and after we were come three Days into the Persian Dominions, we found ourselves oblig'd to part with them; so we gave them three Dollars a Man to go back again.

They understood their Business very well, and knew well enough what was the Reason of it, though we did not. However, we found we had committed a great Mistake in it; for we perceiv'd that they were so exasperated at being turn'd off, that they vowed to be revenged; and, indeed, they had their Revenge to the Full; for the same Day, at Night, they return'd in the Dark, and set eleven Houses on Fire in the Town where we quartered; which, by the Way, had gone near to have cost me my Life, and would certainly have done so, if in the Hurry I had not seiz'd one of the Incendiaries and deliver'd him up to them.

The People were so provok'd at him that was taken that they fell upon him with all possible Fury as the common Incendiary and Burner of the Town, and presently quitted us (for they had before vowed our Destruction) but, as I said, quitted us immediately, and thronged about the Wretch they had taken; and, indeed, I made no Question but that they would have immediately murder'd him (nay, that they would have torn him in Pieces before they parted with him). But after they had vented their Rage at him for some Time with all possible Reproaches and Indignities, they carry'd him before the Cadi, or Judge of the Place. The Cadi, a wise, grave Man, answered, no, he would not judge him at that Time, for they were too hot and passionate to do Justice; but they should come with him in the Morning, when they were cool, and he would hear them.

It is true this was a most excellent Step of the Cadi as to the right Way of doing Justice; but it did not prove the most expedient in the present Occasion, though that was none of his Fault neither; for in the Night the Fellow got out of their Hands, by what Means or by whose Assistance I never heard to this Day; and the Cadi fined the Town in a considerable Sum for letting a Man accused of a capital Crime make his Escape before he was adjudged, and, as we call it, discharged according to Law.

This was an eminent Instance of the Justice of these People; and though they were doubly enraged at the Escape of the Fellow, who, without Doubt, was guilty, yet they never open'd their Mouths against the Cadi; but acquiesc'd in his Judgment, as in that of an Oracle, and submitted to the national Censure, or Censure according to the Custom of their Nation, which he had pass'd upon them in their publick Capacity for the Escape of the Man.

We were willing to get out of this Place as soon as we could; for we found the Peoples Rage, which wanted an Object to vent itself upon, began to threaten us again: So having pack'd up our Goods, and gotten five ordinary Camel-Drivers for our Servants in the Country, we set out again.

The Roads in Persia are not so much frequented, as to be well accommodated with Inns, so that several Times we were oblig'd to lodge upon the Ground in the Way; but our new Servants took Care to furnish us with Lodging; for as soon as we let them know we wanted Rest, and inclin'd to stop, they set up a Tent for us, in so short a Time, that we were scarce able to imagine it possible, and under this we encamp'd, our Camels being just by us, and our Servants and Bales lying all hard by.

Once or twice we lodg'd in publick Inns, built at the King of Persia's Charge: These are fair large Buildings, built square, like a large Inn, they have all of them large Stables, and good Forrage for the Camels and Horses, and Apartments for perhaps two or three hundred People, and they are call'd Caravansera's, as being built to entertain whole Caravans of Travellers: On the great Roads to Tauris and the Side of Turky they are all fortify'd, and are able to entertain five or six Thousand People, and have a Stock to furnish what Number of Men can come with Provisions; nay, it has been known, that whole armies of the Persians have on their March been furnish'd with Provisions in one of these Caravansera's, and that they have kill'd 2000 Sheep for them in one Night's Time.

In this Manner we travell'd to Ispahan, the Capital of Persia, where appearing as Merchants, and with several Camels loaden with Merchandize, we pass'd all Possibility of Suspicion, and being perfectly easy, we continu'd here some Time, sold our Cargoes, and would gladly have remitted the Money to other Places, as for Constantinople in particular; but we found the Turks and Persians have no such Thing as an Exchange, by Bills running between them and other Nations, no, nor between one Town and another.

We were invited here by a sudden Accident to have gone Home by the Caspian Sea and Astracan, so thro' Muscovy; but I had heard so much of the Barbarity of the Russians, the dangerous Navigation of the Caspian Sea by Reason of the Calms and Shoals, the Hazard of being robb'd by the Tartars on the River Wolga, and the like, that I chose to travel to Constantinople, a Journey through Desarts, over Mountains and Wastes, among so many Sorts of Barbarians, that I would run any Kind of Hazards by Sea, before I would attempt such a Thing again.

It would deserve another History to let you into all the different Circumstances of this Journey; how well I was us'd by some, and how ill by others; nay, how well by some Mahometans, how ill by some Christians: But it shall suffice to tell you, that I am at present at Constantinople; and, tho' I write this here, I do not purpose to send it to you till I come to Marseilles in France; from whence I intend to go and live in some inland Town, where, as they have, perhaps, no Notion of the Sea, so they will not be inquisitive after us.

I am, &c.

Daniel Defoe – A Short Biography

Daniel Foe was born around 1660 in Fore Street in the parish of St. Giles Cripplegate in London.

The aristocratic-sounding 'De' was added to his name to create 'Defoe'. On occasion he was prone to claim descent from the family of De Beau Faux.

His father, James Foe, was a prosperous tallow chandler and a member of the Worshipful Company of Butchers and, with Defoe's mother, Annie, Presbyterian dissenters.

Defoe has been born into a time that was rich in dramatic history. In 1665, 70,000 were killed by the Great Plague of London. The following year the Great Fire of London destroyed much of mediaeval London. The Defoe house was one of the few to survive.

In 1667, a third calamity beset London when a Dutch fleet sailed up the Medway via the River Thames and attacked the town of Chatham, as well as destroying much of the British fleet.

By the time Defoe was aged ten accounts suggest his mother, Annie, had died.

Defoe's education began at James Fisher's boarding school in Pixham Lane in Dorking, Surrey. By 14 he was attending a dissenting academy at Newington Green in London run by Charles Morton, and he is then believed to have attended the Newington Green Unitarian Church. During this period, the English government persecuted those who chose to worship outside the Church of England.

Defoe entered the world of business as a general merchant, dealing at different times in hosiery, general woollen goods and wine. His ambitions were great and he was able to buy a country estate, a ship as well as civets, though he was rarely out of debt. (The civet produces an odorous secretion for the purpose of marking out their territory. Diluted, after some time, the odor of civet secretion, normally strong and repulsive, becomes pleasant with animalistic-musk nuance. The animals are kept in cages in order to be able to collect the secretions and thence perfume).

In 1684, Defoe married Mary Tuffley, the daughter of a London merchant, and received a dowry of £3,700 – a huge amount by the standards of the day. With his debts and political difficulties, the marriage may have been troubled, but it lasted 50 years.

In 1685, Defoe joined the ill-fated Monmouth Rebellion but gained a pardon, by which he escaped the Bloody Assizes of the notorious Judge George Jeffreys.

The Glorious Revolution brought Queen Mary and her husband William III to the crown in 1688, and Defoe became one of William's close allies and a secret agent. Some of the new Government policies led to conflict with France, thus damaging many of Defoe's trade relationships.

In 1692, Defoe was arrested for debts of £700 and his civets were taken away. His actual debts are thought to have been nearer £17,000. His laments were loud and he always sided with debtors, but there is evidence that his financial dealings were always above board.

With a wife and seven children to support it was essential that his release was quickly enabled. He achieved this and accounts then suggest he travelled to Europe and Scotland, perhaps to re-establish some business relationships and to trade wine.

By 1695, he was back in England, serving as a "commissioner of the glass duty", and responsible for collecting the tax on bottles. The following year, 1696, he ran a tile and brick factory in what is now Tilbury in Essex and the family lived in the parish of Chadwell St Mary.

Defoe's first notable publication was not one of his great fiction works but a series of proposals for social and economic improvements, a subject for which he had a keen eye and many ideas. An Essay upon Projects was published in 1697.

His most successful poem, The True-Born Englishman (1701), defended the king against the perceived xenophobia of his enemies, satirising the English claim to racial purity. That same year Defoe presented the Legion's Memorial to the Speaker of the House of Commons and later his employer, Robert Harley, flanked by a guard of sixteen gentlemen of quality. It demanded the release of the Kentish petitioners, who had asked Parliament to support the king in an imminent war against France.

In 1702 the death of William III once more created a political crisis. Queen Anne immediately began an attack against Non-conformists. Defoe was one of the first targets. His pamphleteering and political activities quickly resulted in his arrest. This seemed mainly predicated on his December 1702 pamphlet; The Shortest-Way with the Dissenters; Or, Proposals for the Establishment of the Church, which argued for their extermination. In it, he ruthlessly satirised both the High church Tories and those Dissenters who hypocritically practised so-called "occasional conformity". Although it was published anonymously, the Defoe's authorship was quickly unmasked and he was arrested and charged with seditious libel. In fact, Defoe's ironic writing had been misinterpreted, but, alas for him, his trial was to be at the Old bailey in front of the sadistic judge Salathiel Lovell.

Lovell sentenced him to a punitive fine of 200 marks, to public humiliation in a pillory at Charing Cross and an indeterminate length of imprisonment at the Queen's pleasure which would cease only on payment of the enormous fine.

This was an awful moment for Defoe. After his three days in the pillory, he was imprisoned at Newgate.

In despair, he wrote to William Paterson, the London Scot and founder of the Bank of England and who was in the confidence of Robert Harley, 1st Earl of Oxford and Earl Mortimer, a leading minister and spymaster in the English Government. Harley arranged Defoe's release, in 1703, in exchange for Defoe's co-operation as an intelligence agent for the Tories. In exchange for such co-operation with the rival political side, Harley paid some of Defoe's very large outstanding debts, which greatly improved his financial situation.

With his release from Newgate Defoe had, within a few days, witnessed the Great Storm of November 26th, 1703. It caused immense damage to an area from London to Bristol, uprooting millions of trees, and claiming the lives of over 8,000 people, mostly at sea. This became the subject of The Storm (1704), which included many eye-witness accounts and is regarded as one of the world's first examples of modern journalism.

In the same year, he set up his periodical A Review of the Affairs of France which supported the Harley Ministry, and chronicled the events of the War of the Spanish Succession (1702–1714). The Review initially ran weekly but was soon being printed three times a week. Defoe wrote most of the articles himself and although in effect the Review was a Government publication Defoe was enthusiastic and energetic as ever.

Harley was ousted from the ministry in 1708, but Defoe continued writing the Review to support a new master, Godolphin, then again to support Harley and his return in the Tory ministry of 1710–1714. The Tories fell from power with the death of Queen Anne, but Defoe continued his work, now for the Whig government, writing 'Tory' pamphlets that undermined the Tory point of view.

Not all of Defoe's pamphlet writing was political. One pamphlet was originally published anonymously, entitled 'A True Relation of the Apparition of One Mrs. Veal the Next Day after her Death to One Mrs. Bargrave at Canterbury the 8th of September, 1705.' It deals with the crossover between the spiritual and physical realms and describes Mrs. Bargrave's encounter with her old friend Mrs. Veal after she had died.

In 1709, Defoe authored a rather lengthy book entitled The History of the Union of Great Britain. The book attempts to explain the facts leading up to the Act of Union 1707, dating all the way back to December 6th, 1604 when King James was presented with a proposal for unification. (It should be remembered that since the death of Queen Elizabeth England and Scotland, although separate kingdoms, had a common monarch; known as James I of England and as James VI of Scotland. The act now brought the two countries into one; Great Britain.

Part of Defoe's duties as a Government spokesman and spy was the relaying of the Governments view to the public. He thought that his work on the Review would end the threat from the north and gain for the Treasury an "inexhaustible treasury of men", a valuable new market increasing the power of England, clearly the senior partner in the Union. In September 1706, Harley ordered Defoe to Edinburgh to do everything he could to secure loyalty to the Treaty of Union. Defoe was conscious of the risk he was taking. His reports were often vivid descriptions of violent demonstrations against the Union. "A Scots rabble is the worst of its kind", he reported.

Defoe was a Presbyterian who had suffered in England for his convictions, and as such he was accepted as an adviser to the General Assembly of the Church of Scotland and committees of the Parliament of Scotland with little problem.

Defoe received little in the way of reward or recognition from his pay-masters or the government. However, like any good writer, the experiences would be filed away for later use. The Scottish experience was helpful when he came to write his Tour Thro' the Whole Island of Great Britain, published in 1726.

Defoe continued to keep up a wide and varied output including in his apologia Appeal to Honour and Justice (1715), a defence of his part in Harley's Tory ministry (1710–14), The Family Instructor (1715), a conduct manual on religious duty; Minutes of the Negotiations of Monsr. Mesnager (1717), in which he impersonates Nicolas Mesnager, who negotiated the Treaty of Utrecht (1713); and A Continuation of the Letters Writ by a Turkish Spy (1718), a satire of European politics and religion, written by Defoe in the guise of a Muslim in Paris.

From this point Defoe would now enter a period of writing that would cement his place in the canon of English fiction. From 1719 to 1724, Defoe published the novels for which he is now world-famous including Robinson Crusoe in 1719 and Moll Flanders in 1724 amongst many others.

In the final decade of his life, he also wrote conduct manuals, including Religious Courtship (1722), The Complete English Tradesman (1726) and The New Family Instructor (1727).

Defoe seemed to have a natural knack of writing across a wide range of subjects and from a number of points of view. He published on the breakdown of the social order; The Great Law of Subordination Considered (1724) and Everybody's Business is Nobody's Business (1725), together with works on the supernatural; The Political History of the Devil (1726), A System of Magick (1727) and An Essay on the History and Reality of Apparitions (1727). His works on foreign travel and trade include A General History of Discoveries and Improvements (1727) and Atlas Maritimus and Commercialis (1728). Perhaps his greatest achievement is the magisterial A Tour Thro' the Whole Island of Great Britain (1724–27), which provided a panoramic survey of British trade on the eve of the Industrial Revolution.

Published in 1726, The Complete English Tradesman is a late example of Defoe's political and social work. He discusses the role of the tradesman in England in comparison to those abroad, arguing that the British system of trade is far superior. He also states that trade is the backbone of the British economy: "estate's a pond, but trade's a spring."

Defoe was obviously keenly aware of both political and economic structures. Trade, Defoe argues, is a much better vehicle for social and economic change than war. He states that through imperialism and trade expansion the British empire is able to "increase commerce at home" through job creation and increased consumption. This increased consumption, by laws of supply and demand, increases production which in turn raises wages for the poor therefore lifting part of British society further out of poverty.

Daniel Defoe died on April 24th, 1731. Some accounts say that it was whilst hiding from his creditors. Indeed, Defoe was known to enjoy walking on a Sunday when, legally, it was the only day of the week when he could not be legally pestered about his bills. The cause of his death was given as lethargy, but it is thought it was more probably a stroke.

He was interred in Bunhill Fields, London. A monument was erected to his memory there in 1870.

There are various suggestions as to the number of works in Defoe's literary output. Certainly, no less than 200 separate pieces but accounts suggest perhaps as many as 500 which seems, even for so prolific a writer as Defoe, rather too generous but perhaps is in keeping with the extravagance of his life.

Daniel Defoe – A Concise Bibliography

Defoe wrote an immense amount of works. Some were under pseudonyms or anonymously and others may merely have been attributed to him. The list below is by no means exhaustive but is certainly illustrative of both his range and scope.

Novels
Robinson Crusoe (1719)
The Farther Adventures of Robinson Crusoe (1719)
Serious Reflections During the Life and Surprising Adventures of Robinson Crusoe; With His Vision of the Angelic World (1720)

Captain Singleton (1720)
Memoirs of a Cavalier (1720)
A Journal of the Plague Year (1722)
Colonel Jack (1722)
Moll Flanders (1722)
Roxana: The Fortunate Mistress (1724)
Memoirs of a Cavalier: A Military Journal of the Wars in Germany, and the Wars in England.: From the Year 1632 to the Year 1648 (1724)
A New Voyage Round the World (1725)
Military Memoirs of Capt. George Carleton (1728)
A General History of the Pyrates, From their First Rise and Settlement in the Island of Providence, to the Present Time (1724)
The History of the Pyrates (1728)
Of Captain Misson and his Crew (1728)

Essays, Satires & Other Pieces
An Essay Upon Projects (1697)
The Shortest Way with the Dissenters (1702)
New Test of Church of England's Loyalty (1702)
Ode to the Athenian Society (1703)
Enquiry into Acgill's General Translation (1703)
The Storm– a description of the worst storm to hit Britain in recorded times, which includes eyewitness accounts. (1704)
The Great Law of Subordination Consider'd (1704)
Layman's Sermon on the Late Storm (1704)
Elegy on Author of 'True–Born Englishman,' (1704)
Hymn to Victory (1704)
An Essay on the Regulation of the Press (1704)
Giving Alms No Charity (1704)
The Consolidator or, Memoirs of Sundry Transactions from the World in the Moon (1705)
A True Relation of the Apparition of Mrs. Veal (1706)
Sermon on the Filling-up of Dr. Burgess's Meeting-house (1706)
History of the Union of Great Britain (1709)
Atalantis Major (1711)
A Short narrative of the Life and Actions of His Grace John, Duke of Marlborough (1711)
A Seasonable Warning and Caution Against the Insinuations of Papists and Jacobites in Favour of the Pretender (1712)
Short Enquiry into a Late Duel (1713)
A General History of Trade (1713)
An Answer to a Question That Nobody Thinks of, VIZ. But What if the Queen should die? (1713)
Reasons Against the Succession of the House of Hanover with an Enquiry How far the Abdication of King James, Supposing it to be Legal, Ought to Affect the Person of the Pretender (1713)
Wars of Charles III. (1715)
The Family Instructor (1715)
Hymn to the Mob (1715)
The Family Instructor (1715)

An Appeal to Honour and Justice, Though It Be of His Worst Enemies: Being A True Account of His Conduct in Public Affairs (1715)

A Friendly Epistle by Way of Reproof from one of the People Called Quakers, to T. B., a Dealer in Many Words (1715)

Memoirs of the Church of Scotland (1717)

Life and Death of Count Patkul (1717)

Memoirs of the Church of Scotland (1717)

Memoirs of Major Alexander Ramkins (1718)

Memoirs of Duke of Shrewsbury (1718)

Memoirs of Daniel Williams (1718)

A Vindication of the Press (1718)

Dickory Cronke: The Dumb Philosopher: or, Great Britain's Wonder (1719)

The King of Pirates (Capt. Avery) (1719)

Life of Baron de Goertz (1719)

Life and Adventures of Duncan Campbell (1720)

Mr. Campbell's Pacquet (1720)

The Supernatural Philosopher; or, The Mysteries of Magick (1720)

Due Preparations for the Plague (1722)

Life of Cartouche (1722)

Religious Courtship (1722)

History of Peter the Great (1723)

The Highland Rogue (Rob Roy) (1723)

Narrative of Murders at Calais (1724)

The History of The Remarkable Life of John Sheppard (1724)

A Narrative of All The Robberies, Escapes, &c. of John Sheppard (1724)

A Tour Thro' the Whole Island of Great Britain, Divided into Circuits or Journies (1724–1727)

The Great Law of Subordination; or, the Insolence and Insufferable Behaviour of Servants in England (1724)

Account of Jonathan Wild (1725)

Account of John Gow (1725)

Every-body's Business, Is No-body's Business (1725)

The Complete English Tradesman (1725; volume II, 1727)

The Friendly Demon (1726)

Mere Nature Delineated (Peter the Wild Boy) (1726)

Essay upon Literature and the Original of Letters (1726)

History of Discoveries (1726–7)

A System of Magic (1726)

The Protestant Monastery (1726)

The Political History of the Devil (1726)

An Essay Upon Literature (1726)

Mere Nature Delineated (1726)

Conjugal Lewdness (1727)

Treatise concerning Use and Abuse of Marriage (1727)

Secrets of Invisible World Discovered; or, History and Reality of Apparitions (1727)

Parochial Tyranny (1727)

A New Family Instructor (1728)

Augusta Triumphans: or, The Way to Make London the Most Flourishing City in the Universe (1728)

Plan of English Commerce (1728)

Second Thoughts are Best (on Street Robberies) (1728)
Street Robberies Considered (1728)
A Plan of the English Commerce (1728)
Humble Proposal to People of England for Increase of Trade, &c. (1729)
Preface to R. Dodsley's Poem 'Servitude' (1729)
Effectual Scheme for Preventing Street Robberies (1731)

Works in Verse
A New Discovery of an Old Intreague (1691)
Character of Dr. Samuel Annesley (1697)
The Pacificator (1700)
The True-Born Englishman: A Satyr (1701)
Reformation of Manners (1702)
The Mock Mourners (1702)
More Reformation (1703)
Hymn to the Pillory (1703)
The Dyet of Poland (1705)
Jure Divino. A Satyr in 12 books. (1706)
Caledonia (1706)
Translation of Du Fresnoy's "Compleat Art of Painting" (1720)

Printed in Great Britain
by Amazon